T0305870

A REFERENCE MANUAL FOR DATA PRIVACY LAWS AND CYBER FRAMEWORKS

As the world is becoming more digital and entwined together, the cybersecurity threat landscape has no doubt become a daunting one. For example, typical threat variants of the past, especially those of phishing, have now become much more sophisticated and covert in nature. A lot of this has been brought on by the proliferation of ransomware, which exploded during the COVID-19 pandemic. Now, there is another concern that is looming on the horizon: data privacy. Now, more than ever, consumers on a global basis want to know exactly what is happening to their personal identifiable information (PII) datasets. Examples of what they want to know about include the following:

- What kinds and types of information and data are being collected about them.
- How those PII datasets are being stored, processed, and transacted with.
- How their PII datasets are being used by third-party suppliers.

In response to these concerns and fears, as well as the cyber risks posed by these datasets, many nations around the world have set up rather extensive and very detailed data privacy laws. In their respective tenets and provisions, these pieces of legislation not only specify why and how businesses need to comply with them, but also outline the rights that are afforded to each and every consumer. In this book, we detail the tenets and provisions of three key data privacy laws:

- The GDPR
- The CCPA
- The CMMC

We also provide a general framework at the end on how a business can comply with these various data privacy laws.

The book begins with an in-depth overview of the importance of data and datasets, and how they are so relevant to the data privacy laws just mentioned.

Ravindra Das is a technical writer in the cybersecurity realm. He also does cybersecurity consulting on the side through his private practice, M L Tech, Inc. He also holds the Certified in Cybersecurity credential from the ISC(2).

For more information about the series: https://www.routledge.com/
Cyber-Shorts/book-series/CYBSH

A REFERENCE MANUAL FOR DATA PRIVACY LAWS AND CYBER FRAMEWORKS

Ravindra Das

CRC Press
Taylor & Francis Group
Boca Raton London New York

CRC Press is an imprint of the
Taylor & Francis Group, an **informa** business

Designed cover image: © Shutterstock

First edition published 2025
by CRC Press
2385 NW Executive Center Drive, Suite 320, Boca Raton FL 33431

and by CRC Press
4 Park Square, Milton Park, Abingdon, Oxon, OX14 4RN

CRC Press is an imprint of Taylor & Francis Group, LLC

© 2025 Ravindra Das

Library of Congress Cataloging-in-Publication Data
Names: Das, Ravindra, author.
Title: A reference manual for data privacy laws and cyber frameworks / Ravindra Das.
Description: First edition. | Boca Raton : CRC Press, 2025. | Series: Cyber shorts | Includes bibliographical references and index.
Identifiers: LCCN 2024022083 (print) | LCCN 2024022084 (ebook) | ISBN 9781032802428 (hardback) | ISBN 9781032804491 (paperback) | ISBN 9781003496915 (ebook)
Subjects: LCSH: Computer security--Law and legislation--United States. | Computer security--Law and legislation--European Union countries. | Cyberspace--Security measures--United States. | Cyberspace--Security measures--European Union countries. | Data privacy--United States. | Data privacy--European Union countries. | Data protection--Law and legislation--United States. | Data protection--Law and legislation--European Union countries. | COVID-19 Pandemic, 2020---United States. | COVID-19 Pandemic, 2020---European Union countries. | European Parliament. General Data Protection Regulation.
Classification: LCC K3264.C65 D35 2025 (print) | LCC K3264.C65 (ebook) | DDC 343.2409/995--dc23/eng/20240527
LC record available at https://lccn.loc.gov/2024022083
LC ebook record available at https://lccn.loc.gov/2024022084

ISBN: 978-1-032-80242-8 (hbk)
ISBN: 978-1-032-80449-1 (pbk)
ISBN: 978-1-003-49691-5 (ebk)

DOI: 10.1201/9781003496915

Typeset in Caslon
by SPi Technologies India Pvt Ltd (Straive)

*This book is dedicated to my Lord and Savior, Jesus
Christ, the Grand Designer of the Universe, and to my
parents, Dr. Gopal Das and Mrs. Kunda Das.
And to my loving cats, Fifi and Bubu
This book is also dedicated to:
Richard and Gwynda Bowman
Jaya Chandra
Tim Auckley
Patricia Bornhofen
Ashish Das*

Contents

Acknowledgments

I would like to thank Ms. Gabrielle Williams, my editor, who made this book into a reality.

1

INTRODUCTION AND A
REVIEW OF DATA SCIENCE

In the world of business, there is one major lifeline that all organizations primarily depend upon: the data they store, process, and archive. These datasets can be just about anything. For example, it could be competitive intelligence of your industry or it could even be information about your customers and employees. Data stored like this is very often referred to as "Personal Identifiable Information Datasets", more commonly known as "PII datasets". A technical definition of this is as follows:

> Personally identifiable information (PII) is any information connected to a specific individual that can be used to uncover that individual's identity, such as their social security number, full name, email address or phone number.
>
> *(SOURCE: https://www.ibm.com/topics/pii)*

Or you may have even stored information and data about the buying patterns of your customers. With the help of artificial intelligence (AI), this data can be used to predict future buying patterns, in order for your business to come up with newer and more innovative products and solutions that not only meets the needs of future prospects but keeps you ahead of the competition as well. For example, if you conduct market research, you can even store this kind of data to model future questions to potential customers in focus group interviews.

Another huge example of data storage is in the healthcare industry. In this regard, it is primarily the patients' records that are kept in the databases. This can include everything from the results of certain tests that have been conducted to the minutes from telehealth

DOI: 10.1201/9781003496915-1   **1** appointments and actual visits with doctors. Also, prescription medication history can be kept as well, which allows healthcare provider to examine past trends in terms of both usage and dosage, and make changes for the future.

The Types of Datasets

But whatever the nature of the datasets is, they typically fall under three broad categories:

1. The Structured Data: In these instances, the datasets are typically well-defined and labeled. It is used in a statistical model that has already been established and configured per the requirements of the project. The attributes of each piece of data, in this regard, are also well defined, and even the meta data is captured. This is simply the "data that describes the data". In other words, these are just dub components of the main pieces of data. For example, if the database contains profiles about individuals, then such data fields, as weight, name, height, birthdate, address, gender, and race, will also be considered as the meta data, because they are describing the attributes of the individual, which, in turn, makes up the entire composite picture of them. Other primary examples of meta data include the following:
   - Currencies
   - Geo location, such as latitude and longitude
   - Credit card numbers
   - Transaction information, such as purchases and deposits and/or withdrawals that have been made from a bank account

   It is important to note that structured data is primarily quantitative-based, as exemplified in the examples. Because of this, pretty much anyone can infer what the data means and what it is about. But how exactly it will be used depends upon the application or project in question.

   Also, structured data is typically arranged in a tabular format. In these instances, the columns represent the attributes and each row represents the record. The end result is the intersection of the column and row, which is technically referred to as a "cell". This contains the value about that attribute for that particular record.

2. The Unstructured Data: This is also referred to as "unstructured data". In these instances, the datasets are not nearly as clearly defined as the structured datasets. In other words, human intervention is often required to ascertain as to what a particular piece of data signifies. Examples of these kinds of datasets include the following:

   • Images (human and machine-generated)
   • Video files
   • Audio files
   • Social media posts

It should even be mentioned here that Email messages can be considered as unstructured data. The primary reason for this is that they too contain meta data, such as the date the data was sent and received, the Email address, and name of the sender.

As mentioned, although human intervention is still needed in these kinds of datasets, generative AI is now gaining the ability to actually decipher the types of files as mentioned earlier. This is primarily driven by the fact that it is the GPT4 algorithms that are being used. For example, ChatGPT (possibly the most widely used generative AI tool now) can not only be fed these kinds of datasets, but can also, to varying degrees, be created as outputs in response to a query that has been submitted to it.

3. The Big Data: These kinds of datasets can be technically defined as follows:

   Big data refers to extremely large and diverse collections of structured, unstructured, and semi-structured data that continues to grow exponentially over time. These datasets are so huge and complex in volume, velocity, and variety, that traditional data management systems cannot store, process, and analyze them.

   (SOURCE: https://cloud.google.com/learn/what-is-big-data)

Notice that in the above definition, there are three key terms that also need to be defined, and they are as follows:

- <u>Volume</u>: These are datasets which contain enormous quantities of information. As a result, high demands are placed on devices for storing, manipulating, and processing them.
- <u>Variety</u>: This simply refers to servers and databases that process datasets from many sources: These include emails, images, video, audio, log files from IoT devices, PDF documents, and so on. As a result, these huge swings in the types and kinds of data files can pose issues when storing data and extracting information.
- <u>Velocity</u>: With the power of generative AI, huge quantities of information and data are being generated at literally the blink of an eye. As a result, business managers have to make split-second decisions on the courses of action that they need to take into the future. This rapid fire presentation of data, its analysis, and quick decision making that is needed is referred to as "velocity".

These three concepts are illustrated in Figure 1.1:

Figure 1.1

(SOURCE: https://www.shutterstock.com/image-vector/big-data-banner-web-icon-flat-1113268736/edit?chatId=274ac4f217ce4420821bffcd3138a244)

The Kinds of Data Models

The Relational Data Model

Now that we have presented three main types of data categories, it is now important to review the kinds of models that they can be used in. Broadly speaking, there are two areas for this:

- Artificial intelligence
- Statistical models

With regard to AI, models can be created that are quite simple or even very complex. They can fall into the following categories:

*Machine learning
*Neural networks
*Advanced neural networks
*Computer vision
*Generative AI
*Large language models (also referred to as LLMs)

Much more detail about the kinds and types of models that can be created in the aforementioned categories can be seen in two books about AI that we have published:

"Practical AI For Cybersecurity"
https://www.routledge.com/Practical-AI-for-Cybersecurity/
    Das/p/book/9780367437152
"Generative AI: Phishing And Cybersecurity Metrics"

In terms of the latter, the following are the categories that can be created to store and process datasets:

1. The Relational Data Model: This is where the datasets are organized into tables known as "relations". These comprise rows and columns. The rows are also technically referred to as "tuples". They consist of a series of related data values. In this regard, the columns are technically referred to as the "attributes". Their primary purpose is to describe what those specific values are.

   A typical example of this is a student roster, and is illustrated in the example below:

Student ID #	Last Name	Email	Phone #	Age	Geo Location
323232	Jones	tracey@ii.com	6304212522	55	Chicago, IL
323233	Bowman	rich@aol.com	4142657350	45	Carbondale, IL
323234	Ryniec	jill@hotmail.com	6304788921	52	Louisville, KY
323235	Das	ravi@yahoo.com	6304652603	55	New York City

Figure 1.2

It is important to note that there are three distinct properties of the relational data model, and they are as follows:

- <u>Data Structure</u>: This is a set a mathematical set of relationships which clearly define how the datasets can be represented.
- <u>Data Manipulation</u>: This refers to how the datasets can be made so that it is easier to analyze, which, in turn, will result in less overhead in terms of processing and computing resources.
- <u>Data Integrity</u>: These are the rules and permutations that define how the datasets remain intact in order to confirm their validity.

The Advantages and Disadvantages

The relational data model has a number of key advantages, which are as follows:

1. <u>Greater Levels of Scalability</u>: It can be easily scaled up or down as needed and per your requirements, as they change over time. For instance, if you need to add more data to a table, you can quickly add in a new column. This scalability function can also be further realized if the relational model is used in a cloud-based environment, such as the AWS or Microsoft Azure.
2. <u>Greater Structure</u>: A relational data model can also enforce integrity, consistency, among all of your datasets that are stored in it.

But along with these strategic advantages also come the disadvantages. They are as follows:

1. <u>A Greater Degree of Inflexibility</u>: Although relational data models do offer scalability, it can only be reached up to a certain point. For example, if you have many of them interconnected, making a change in one will have a cascading effect on the other models. This could lead to a huge deterioration in performance and optimization, and it could also take a great deal of time to try to pinpoint of what exactly went wrong.
2. <u>A Slower Effect</u>: While it is true that a relational data model can store large amounts of data, if too many queries are placed upon it, it can also slow down the performance of it.

For example, one model may have to cross-reference others in order to properly answer your query. This can also lead to degradation by taking up too much compute and processing powers, as well as bandwidth.

3. Complex: It is a known fact that relational data models can also become very complex, as they store and transact more datasets. The Structured Query Language (also known as SQL) will need to be continually reformulated as demands further increase on the relational data models.

The Hierarchical Data Model

This kind of model is specifically designed to organize and categorize datasets into a specialized kind of hierarchy. The perfect example of this is the family tree. The parent record is technically referred to as the "root node", and anything below this is known as "child node", connected by various linkages. The only caveat here is that there can only be one parent node for each child node, but the parent node can have multiple levels or "layers" of child nodes.

In the illustration depicted earlier, the root node is "electronics devices". There are two "child nodes" which are the wireless devices and the portable devices. In turn, these also act as "parent categories" by having their own child nodes. For example, under "wireless devices", namely the "iOS devices" and the "android devices". But, it is important to keep in mind that these directories, also known as "records", fall under one single parent, which is the root node.

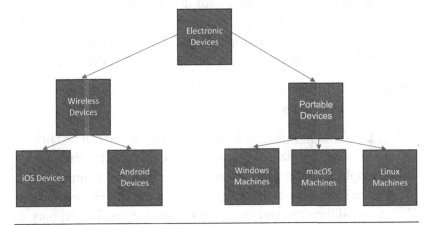

Figure 1.3

The Advantages and Disadvantages

The hierarchical data model has a number of key advantages, which are as follows:

1. Ease of Understanding: The hierarchical data model exactly mirrors how human beings organize information and data in their minds. As a result, this kind of model is a natural fit for many kinds of applications, such as databases, file systems, and document management systems.

2. Greater Levels of Performance: If the data is contained in a hierarchical structure, the end user can gain access to information with a single operation. When compared to the relational data models, this is a much more efficient process than having to retrieve data from separate tables, even though they may all be linked together.

3. Easier Levels of Maintenance: Since all of the data are stored in a one, single table, there is no need to keep track of multiple tables. This way, the data can be kept consistently across the entire system in real time.

4. Breakdown of Complex Information: Because the hierarchical data model distills complex information into smaller and more manageable pieces, it easier to work with and manipulate large amounts of data.

5. Access Different Bits of Data: This kind of model supports the functionality of the multiple views of data. This becomes especially important for those kinds of environments that need to provide different end users with different views of the same information. For example, a hierarchical data model could allow managers to see employee data in a hierarchical structure. The employees could see the same data in a flat structure.

But along with these strategic advantages also come the disadvantages. They are as follows:

1. A Limited Flexibility: A hierarchical data model can be fairly rigid, since the data is organized in a treelike structure. For example, if you need to add or subtract data, the entire structure will have to be reconfigured. As a result, this can make it very difficult to construct and deploy queries. The primary

reason for this is that you need to follow the path again throughout the hierarchy to compute the desired output.

2. <u>A Large Amount of Duplication</u>: In the hierarchical data model, the child nodes very often contain duplicate records of the data that are stored in the parent nodes. This can lead to inconsistency and data sprawl in the model, which can greatly degrade performance and optimization of the system.

The Network Data Model

The network data model is another hierarchy of data, but when compared to the model just previously described, it consists of a much more flexible series of relationships and linkages. The main difference is that the nodes in this kind of model can have multiple parent nodes instead of just one of them.

In the network data models, the parents are technically known as the "owners". Also, the data points that form the next level down in the hierarchy are called "members". As a result, they allow for more flexibility and complexity in the linkages between data points.

An example of a network data model is illustrated as follows:

The Advantages and Disadvantages

The network data model has a number of key advantages, which are as follows:

1. <u>Complex Relationships Can Be Presented</u>: The network data models can express both simple and complex relationships among the data points. For example, they can capture data with a one-to-many structure (mathematically represented as "1:1") and many-to-many structure (mathematically represented as "N:N").

2. <u>There Is Simplified Database Management</u>: Just like the other models just examined, network data models are simple and logical to create, design, deploy, and implement.

3. <u>More Efficient Ways of Creating Queries</u>: Any changes that are made to the parent data are automatically transmitted and reflected in the child data. As a result, this makes it easier to make changes to batches of data of all types and kinds. It is

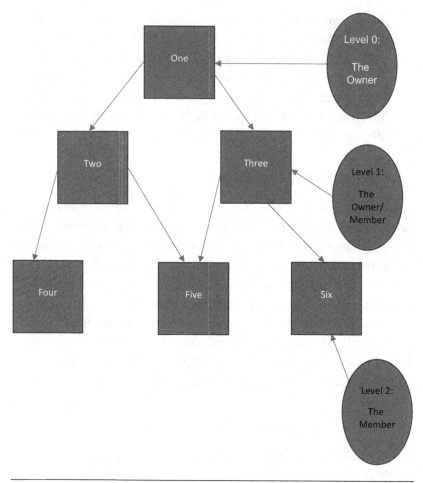

Figure 1.4

important to note that making structural changes to the network data model is complex. The primary reason for this is that datasets are so interconnected with another that if you need to modify a certain set of data, you'll also need to track down and correspondingly change all the other datasets that are also connected to it.

4. Improved Rates in Retrieving Data: A very unique feature of the network data model is that it can create multiple pathways through the interconnected relationships among the data points. As a result, it can be easier for the end user to access the needed data.

5. <u>Easy to Understand</u>: It is also important to note that the network data model can be used to capture the linkages or the interrelationships that exist between the datasets in different, innovative, and creative ways.

But along with these strategic advantages, also come the disadvantages. They are as follows:

1. <u>There Is Limited Scalability</u>: The network data model has far less scalability than the other models. The primary reason for this is that the relationships between datasets can become more complex as the database(s) grows.
2. <u>Can Be Harder to Query</u>: When a query is deployed into a network data model, it can be challenging to get the desired output, because the relationships between datasets are more complex and can be difficult to understand.
3. <u>No Flexibility</u>: Finally, a network data model is not as flexible as other models, such as the relational model. This means that it is far more difficult to make changes to the datasets and their corresponding structures without affecting and impacting the overall structure and integrity of the database.

The Types of Data Analysis

So far in this chapter, we have extensively reviewed the major datasets and the types of models that can be used to further analyze and manipulate them. But, once you have collected the datasets, you need to have a way of analyzing them in order to interpret what they really mean for your query. For example, if a threat researcher has collected all of the information and data that he or she needs, then they need some kind of analysis technique in order to get to the answer that they are looking for.

For example, if they are trying to model a new threat variant based on previous signature profiles, they will need a technique to manipulate and analyze all of the information and data they have collected in order to find that answer. For example, if they have datasets A, B, C, and D, they will need to analyze all of them in order to come up with a conclusion, which is what threat variant "F" will look like in the future. In this section, we will closely examine some of the major statistical analysis that one can embark upon in order to find the answer to their specific query.

The Descriptive Analysis

Simply put, this particular technique examines what has happened in the past. If you have a very small dataset, this can be a relatively easy task to do with a spreadsheet. But if you have lots of data, then you will need an automated tool to conduct this task, and in this regard, generative AI, neural networks, and even machine learning would be great options to use.

The primary purpose of descriptive analytics is to simply describe what has happened. In other words, it does not look for a cause and effect type of relationship, nor does it try to explain why certain event might have happened. The goal is to merely provide a snapshot of all of the data and information that have been collected, which can be more or less easily understood.

In this regard, there are two main techniques that are used to conduct a descriptive analysis project. They are as follows:

1. Data Aggregation: This is the process of gathering all of the datasets and tabulating them into a summary-like format. A prime example of this is an online merchant. They will obviously collect all kinds of information and data relating to their customers and prospects who either visit their website or make and actual purchase from their online store. In this instance, the aggregated data will be a summary of a particular variable of interest, such as the average number of purchases made, and their corresponding dollar amount.

Data Mining

If the end user wants to use descriptive analysis to take their summary (as just described) one step further, then the tool they would use here is called "data mining". It can be technically defined as follows:

Data mining is a computer-assisted technique used in analytics to process and explore large data sets. With data mining tools and methods, organizations can discover hidden patterns and relationships in their data. Data mining transforms raw data into practical knowledge. Companies use this knowledge to solve problems, analyze the future impact of business decisions, and increase their profit margins.

(SOURCE: https://aws.amazon.com/what-is/data-mining/)

Simply put, this is where the data scientist will apply various statistical techniques in order to find trends that could further substantiate the aggregation summary, as described. For example, if a threat researcher has enough information and data about previous Malware signature profiles, then through their own experience, they can make an educated guess as to what a future threat variant could possibly look like. But, if they want to further substantiate this, then the tools of data mining will be needed. Another key benefit of data mining is that even unhidden trends can be discovered, which can even be used as intelligence information and data. In this regard, there are four specialized techniques, which are as follows:

- Association Rules: Different rules are deployed to ascertain the relationships between data points in a given dataset.
- Neural Networks: This is a specialized form of artificial intelligence, which was reviewed in our last book entitled: "Generative AI: Phishing and Cybersecurity Metrics". These kinds of algorithms and models process training data and by using different layers of digital nodes, which are also technically referred to as "neurons".
- Decision Trees: The concept of this was reviewed earlier in this chapter. Essentially, use multiple regression methods in order to predict outcomes based on predetermined decisions. This is provided in a treelike visualization so that the outcomes of different decisions can be easily understood. In this regard, multiple regression analysis can be defined as follows:

  Multiple regression is an extension of linear regression models that allow predictions of systems with multiple independent variables.

  (SOURCE: https://builtin.com/data-science/multiple-regression)

A good example of this is used in agricultural economics, for example:

$$OPFI = \beta C1 + \beta SM2 + \beta W3 + \beta B4 + \beta P5 + \beta V6 + \beta M6 + D1 + D2 + D3 + D4$$

where:

OPFI = Optimal pig feed input

C = Corn

SM = Soybean meal

W = Wheat

B = Barley

P = Protein

V = Vitamins

M = Minerals

D1, D2, D3, D4 = Dummy variables

In other words, the agricultural producer is trying to determine the best combination of variables that should be used when creating a specialized type of feed for optimal livestock production.

- <u>K-Nearest Neighbor</u>: These are also technically referred to as the "KNN algorithms". These are primarily used to organize and classify data points based on their closeness and association to other relevant and available data points (which are referred to as the "neighbors"). They can also be used for calculating the distance between data points, especially when the "Euclidean distance" is involved.

It should be noted at this point that the use of data aggregation comes with its own set of advantages and disadvantages. The advantages are as follows:

- Complex data can be easier to understand.
- Only basic mathematical and statistical skills are needed to carry out the required tasks.
- Readily available tools such as Microsoft Excel can be used to carry out the analysis.
- It relies on data that is already in existence; there is no need to source additional datasets.
- It looks at all of the datasets in order to come up with the summary.

The disadvantages are as follows:

- The summary may not tell a complete story of the datasets.
- If you want to test a statistical hypothesis, then you will need to use the techniques of data mining.
- Descriptive analytics may not be the best tool to use to predict what may happen in the future.
- Descriptive analytics does not describe the data and information collection methodology.

Diagnostic Analytics

The primary goal of diagnostic analytics is to do a deep dive in order to understand why something happened. Another main goal of diagnostic analytics is to identify and respond to any anomalies that exist within your datasets.

As it relates to cybersecurity, your IT security team may have set a threshold of three login attempts for the employees to log into their devices. Anything greater than that would for sure signify an unusual pattern, which could be indicative of a malicious intent. The principles of diagnostic analysis can provide greater insight into this.

But, diagnostic analysis can also be used for the greater good. For example, if the goal of the CISO is have their security team detect and respond to threat variants in a quicker time frame, then diagnostic analysis will be useful for computing and quantifying these two key cybersecurity metrics:

- The Mean Time to Detect: This is also referred to as MTTD. This describes how long it takes for the IT security team to detect that an actual security breach is underway.
- The Mean Time to Respond: This is also referred to as MTTR. This describes how long it takes for the IT security team to respond to and contain an actual security breach is underway.

    There are also a number of key techniques that are used in diagnostic analysis, which are as follows:
- Factor Analysis: This is also referred to as "dimension reduction". This specialized technique provides greater insights into why a particular event has actually happened. It does

this by condensing the data into a smaller number of "super variables", which makes the data easier to work with. As it relates to cybersecurity, a threat researcher could group all the information and data that they have collected about the signature profiles of the threat variants into distinct categories, and have one "super variable" that represents each of those particular categories.

- Cohort Analysis: A "cohort" is a grouping of datasets that have a certain characteristics in common within a certain time frame. Once again, a good example of this would be the total number of unsuccessful login attempts over a span of just one month. If there are spikes over certain months, then that is an indicator that a cyberattacker could be trying to penetrate the IT and network infrastructure during off-hours.

- Cluster Analysis: This statistical technique is designed specifically to identify structures within a dataset. In order to do this, it segments the datasets into groups that are "internally homogenous and externally heterogeneous". In other words, this simply means that the data that resides under one "super variable" must be similar to one another, but do not have to be with the other datasets that reside under different "super variables".

  A key advantage of cluster analysis is that you can see how the datasets are distributed among one another. For example, if the total number of unsuccessful login attempts happens at a particular time over certain months, then this can be grouped into one "cluster". These datasets can then be compared to other "clusters", which have differing times of unsuccessful login attempts.

- Time Series Analysis: Time series analysis is the study and analysis of sequential datasets that measure the same variable at different points in time. The main intention here is to collect data at specific intervals over a period of time in order to identify any particular trends and cycles. For example, in cybersecurity, this could be used to calculate the "mean time to detect" to a particular threat variant in a certain month.

- Monte Carlo Methodology: This can be technique that can be defined as follows:

The Monte Carlo simulation is a mathematical technique that predicts possible outcomes of an uncertain event. Computer programs use this method to analyze past data and predict a range of future outcomes based on a choice of action.

(SOURCE: https://aws.amazon.com/what-is/monte-carlo-simulation/)

For example, if you have a generative AI model already deployed, you can feed it the datasets of previous unsuccessful login attempts. From there, you can ask it to predict the total number of unsuccessful login attempts that could take place, for example, during the holiday season, when many employees travel and work remotely. Because of this, the cyberattackers know that their guard will be down and will take full advantage to gain access to the IT and network infrastructure.

It should be noted at this point that the use of diagnostic analysis comes with its own set of advantages and disadvantages. The advantages are as follows:

1. It Improves Decision Making: How much diagnostic analysis can help to improve a businesses' decision-making process is a direct function of the sheer amount of data that they have access to both internally and externally. With the threat researcher, the more of this they have, the better they can predict future threat variants.

2. It Can Increase the Levels of Efficiency: As an example in the Supply Chain/Logistics Industry, predictive analysis increases not only the levels of efficiency by preventing equipment malfunction, but it can also be used to help identify new ways to streamline business transactions, find more optimal routes to deliver products and services, and allow for a business to adjust to dynamic trends even faster.

3. It Improves Risk Management: As mentioned earlier, diagnostic analytics can analyze a huge amount of massive data to detect fraud, detect vulnerabilities in the digital and physical asserts, and so on. All of this, in turn, will help to mitigate the risks of major financial losses. The bottom line is that those businesses that make use of predictive analytics can easily learn

from past mistakes in order to apply what has been learned, and, thus, create a more successful future.

4. <u>It Can Provide Competitive Intelligence</u>: If a single cyber business competes with many others to offer customers the same products and services, using diagnostic analytics can give that particular business an edge over the competition. This is especially true in the Managed Service Provider (MSSP) and Managed Security Service Provider (MSSP) space, as the competition is very high.

5. <u>It Can Help to Improve Supply Chain Management</u>: Predictive analytics can serve the supply chain management by tracking and determining how resources are used and making predictions when they have to be replenished and restocked. This can also aid in "Just In Time Inventory", when the raw supplies and parts are ordered on an as needed basis, without keeping extra inventory on hand.

The disadvantages are as follows:

1. <u>It May Not Be Useful All the Time</u>: Although diagnostic analytics can be used to help make forecasts about future needs and trends, its one flaw is that it cannot predict when events occur instantaneously, such as a massive Supply Chain Attack, as the world saw with the Solar Winds hack.

2. <u>It Needs To Be Updated</u>: A successful Diagnostic Analytics tool needs to be updated with fresh information and data on a regular basis. For example, depending on the industry or application, the datasets from a previous time period earlier may be too outdated to serve any useful purposes for future needs. This is especially true if you are planning to make use of a generative AI model as a predictive analytics tool.

3. <u>You Must Have a Plan</u>: Before you invest the time and resources to deploy diagnostic analytics, you must absolutely have a clear goal and objective in mind that needs to be accomplished. For example, when a business first starts out with predictive analytics, the CISO thinks that simply mining the data will produce valuable insights and/or reveal hidden trends. This kind of thinking and approach can be dangerous, as it may not yield anything insightful and can be a drain on precious resources.

4. <u>Missing Data</u>: In order for a diagnostic analytics tool to work, you have to fully ensure that you have all of the datasets that you need for your query. Any missing data can greatly skew the results and guide you in the wrong direction. The bottom line here is that this can greatly increase your level of risk, especially when it comes to cybersecurity.

5. <u>Inaccurate Data</u>: Also, any datasets that you make use of also have to be extremely accurate so that once again you will yield the correct answer to your query. As it has been mentioned in our previous books on AI, this is extremely critical if you are planning to make use of a generative AI model. Extra time and effort must be taken to fully ensure that the datasets you are making use of for the initial training of the model are cleansed and optimized. But, this is not a one-time thing. Anytime you feed new datasets into the generative AI model, this process must be done all the time. If not, the outputs that are yielded will be highly skewed, as well as highly inaccurate.

Predictive Analytics

As its name implies, predictive analytics aims to predict what is likely to happen in the future, which is largely based on past patterns and trends. This is especially useful as it enables businesses to plan ahead, especially when it comes to cybersecurity. Once again, the best example of this the threat researcher. Apart from simply analyzing what the past signature profiles have looked like, in terms of trends, the other key question is how can the data and information that has been collected in this regard be used to predict future threat variants?

This is where predictive analytics will come into play, especially if generative AI is incorporated into it. By using some facet of AI, many outcomes, especially "What-If Scenarios", can be played out. But apart from just predicting specific threat variants, predictive analytics in this regard can also be used to help predict what the overall cyber threat landscape will look into the future, especially when you factor in nation state threat actors as well.

Apart from forecasting, predictive analytics is also used for classification. A prime example of this is the "logistic regression". This is a specialized statistical technique that is used to predict a binary-based outcome (typically *yes* or *no*) based on an established set of independent variables. A good example of this is a bank, deciding whether to give out or a loan or not to a customer. In this particular instance, logistic regression will be used to predict if this customer will default on the loan or not. The result will be classified into one of two categories: "they will pay back the loan" or "they will not pay back the loan".

Also, there are number of statistical techniques that are used in predictive analytics, which are as follows:

1. The Random Forest: This is deemed to be one of the most sophisticated techniques that is currently available for use in predictive analytics. The primary reason for this is that it makes usage of heavy usage of both decision trees and machine learning. The former was reviewed earlier in this chapter, and the latter was also closely examined in our previous two books on AI.

   Essentially, the logic behind the random forest technique is to use multiple, uncorrelated decision trees and bring them together as one cohesive unit. The premise here is that they will work better as a group rather than themselves individually. By using the random forest technique, each individual decision tree classification is also known as a "vote". The random forest technique will then choose the majority of the votes and, from there, computes an average, which then, in turn, becomes the answer to the query that is presented to it.

   A key line of thinking here is that while individual decision trees produce errors, the majority of them will produce a much more accurate result. Thus, the overall outcome can be computed correctly, ensuring the overall outcome goes in the right direction.

   Since machine learning is a huge component of the random forest, it is very important to review the techniques also that are used when training these kinds of models. They are as follows:

   • The Bootstrap: This uses the techniques of "row sampling" and "feature sampling" in order to create sample datasets from the aggregate ones for every machine model that is being used.

- The Aggregation: This technique further reduces the size of the sample datasets into what are known as "summary statistics". This is also technically known as "bootstrap aggregation", which is used for cutting down on the level of variance that are exhibited in the decision trees.
- The Variance: This is not a technique per se but rather a critical error that results from high levels of sensitivity to small-degree fluctuations that are exhibited in the dataset. As a result, any level of high variance will cause the algorithms in the machine learning model to further exhibit extra "noise" when processing the output. This is technically known as "overfitting".
- The Bagging: This is the specific application of making use of the bootstrap method to further reduce the levels of high variance that is being exhibited by a machine learning algorithm.

Finally, a technical definition of the random forest is as follows:

> Random Forest is a powerful and versatile supervised machine learning algorithm that grows and combines multiple decision trees to create a "forest". It can be used for both classification and regression problems in R and Python.
>
> *(SOURCE: https://careerfoundry.com/en/blog/data-analytics/what-is-random-forest/)*

2. K-Means Clustering: This can be technically defined as follows:

> K-Means Clustering is an Unsupervised Learning algorithm, which groups the unlabeled dataset into different clusters. Here K defines the number of pre-defined clusters that need to be created in the process, as if K=2, there will be two clusters, and for K=3, there will be three clusters, and so on.
>
> *(SOURCE: https://www.javatpoint.com/k-means-clustering-algorithm-in-machine-learning)*

In terms of breaking this definition down, it is important to keep the following concepts in mind:

- An unsupervised learning algorithm is one where virtually no human intervention is required in order to correctly come up with the output.
- An unlabeled dataset is a piece of data that is not assigned a particular category or unique identifier.

    Thus, K-means clustering is used to organize these unlabeled datasets into carefully defined "clusters" so that the machine learning algorithms will be able to process them much more efficiently and effectively.

3. The K-Nearest Neighbor: This is also referred to as the "k-NN". It is technically defined as follows:

> The k-nearest neighbors (KNN) algorithm is a non-parametric, supervised learning classifier, which uses proximity to make classifications or predictions about the grouping of an individual data point.

> *(SOURCE: https://www.ibm.com/topics/knn)*

The important concept that needs to be broken down here is as follows:

- With supervised learning, a lot of human intervention is required in order to correctly come up with the output.

    This technique is used on large sets of training data that are ingested into the machine learning model, where each piece of data in the overall datasets is represented by a series of other variables. It is primarily used to make sure that the datasets which are ingested into the machine learning model for training purposes are processed both effectively and efficiently.

4. The ARIMA Model: This is an acronym that stands for "auto regressive integrated moving average". It is technically defined as follows:

> ARIMA, is a statistical analysis model that uses time series data to either better understand the data set or to predict future trends.

> *(SOURCE: https://www.investopedia.com/terms/a/autoregressive-integrated-moving-average-arima.asp)*

In other words, this technique is used to predict some kind of future event based on what has happened in the past. Probably, the simplest example of this is trying to predict the price of a stock based on previous pricing patterns. This would be an attempt to make a profitable trade at some point in time going in the future.

Further, ARIMA makes use of what is known as "autoregression" and the "moving average", which are used to smoothen out the variance in the time series data. Also, ARIMA models are mainly used in long-term trends or seasonal pattern kinds of applications.

It should be noted at this point that the use of predictive analysis comes with its own set of advantages as well as disadvantages. The advantages are as follows:

1. Quantitative-Based Decision Making: Since predictive analytics uses hard core numbers for the datasets, any team, especially the IT security one, will be able to make much informed decisions based on the insights that have been gleaned from the datasets. As a result, real-time recommendations, forecasts, or key insights can be provided to all of the stakeholders involved in a particular project. Because of this, data-driven decision will also help to create far more effective products and service development.

2. Greater User Experience: From the standpoint of web application development, this is also known as the "UX", which stands for "user experience". Therefore, predictive analytics, embedded within an application, can also provide personalized and context-aware experiences for users, especially where generative AI is involved. For example, by analyzing user behavior and historical data on that end user, a generative AI tool, such as ChatGPT, can proactively suggest relevant content, solutions, and actions that should be taken. The main advantage of this is that not only is end-user satisfaction greatly improved, but it also fosters an environment where end-user engagement and loyalty are totally fostered.

3. Better Uses of Resources: From the standpoint of economic theory, this is also technically known as "resource allocation".

In this regard, predictive analytics can help a procurement team further optimize demand forecasting, identify potential performance bottlenecks, and so on. This is especially needed by the supply chain and logistics industries, particularly when adopting "Just In Time Inventory", which was reviewed earlier in this chapter. Another good example of this is in a cloud deployment. For example, the IT security team can help anticipate uptrends and downtrends for a certain application, and in turn, scale the server capacity accordingly. This helps to avoid over-provisioning and under-provisioning of virtual machine resources.

The disadvantages are as follows:

1. <u>Data Privacy</u>: Predictive analytics requires access to what is known as "personal identifiable information" (also known as PII in short). The technical definition of PII is as follows:

   > Personally identifiable information (PII) is any information connected to a specific individual that can be used to uncover that individual's identity, such as their social security number, full name, email address or phone number.

   > *(SOURCE: https://www.ibm.com/topics/pii)*

   Because of the sensitivity of PII, concerns about data privacy and security have now become mainstream, especially with the use of generative AI. For example, if not properly implemented and secured, predictive models could very well expose confidential information about individuals to unauthorized third parties. As a result, many data privacy laws, such as the GDPR and the CCPA, have been created. The concept of data privacy and these regulations will be explored in this book.

2. <u>An Increased Level of Biasness</u>: As reviewed in this chapter, predictive analytics models, especially those that incorporate generative AI, are only as good as the datasets that they are trained on. If these datasets are not cleansed and optimized, the predictive analytics model will yield inaccurate or biased outputs. This will lead to incorrect recommendations and

could very well reinforce existing biases about generative AI that the end user may already have in their mind.

3. <u>Lack of Trust</u>: The end user could very well feel uncomfortable knowing the fact that a predictive analytics model that makes of generative AI is being used to answer their specific query. In this regard, the sheer lack of transparency and understanding about how the answers to the queries are being generated can quickly erode end-user trust. This in turn will lead to a sharp decrease in the adoption usage of the application. As our previous books on AI have explored, this is also known as the "Back Box Phenomenon". Meaning, there is absolutely no level of transparency being offered as to how the actual output is being computed. Therefore, clear explanations of how all of this is done need to be provided to the end user. Equally important, the end user must be given control over data and privacy settings to keep their PII datasets private and secure.

Prescriptive Analytics

The goal here is to try to examine what has happened in the past and, from there, determine what the next course of action should be. A good example of this is in cybersecurity, when a security breach has impacted a business. After the breach has been contained, the IT security team will try to examine the factors that led to the incident, and from there, try to ascertain a way in which this can be mitigated moving forward in the future.

A technical definition of prescriptive analytics as follows:

Prescriptive analytics is an advanced data analytics model that dives deep into data and offers recommendations and insights on 'what should you do?' to achieve desired outcomes. Unlike descriptive analytics which summarizes historical data and predictive analytics which forecasts future trends, prescriptive analytics goes one step further by suggesting different action plans and showing the implications of each action.

(SOURCE: https://www.thoughtspot.com/data-trends/analytics/
prescriptive-analytics)

But given the advent of generative AI, neural networks, and machine learning, these are the kinds of models that one would want to use to try forecast the future, especially that of generative AI, since it makes use of the most advanced GPT4 algorithms. But before all of this took off last year in 2023, the two main tools that were used for prescriptive analysis are as follows:

1. <u>The Rule-Based Modeling</u>: This is also technically known as "heuristics". They are based on a set of predefined rules and typically involve the use of decision trees, statistics, and other sorts of algorithms reviewed earlier in this chapter to determine the needed answers. However, heuristics are good only for problems and applications that have a very limited scope.

   It is important to note that heuristics, given its limited scope, are comparably easy to understand and deploy. But on the flip side, it can be quite difficult to take into consideration other kinds of constraints that need to be accounted for.

2. <u>The Linear Programming</u>: This is also known as "optimization modeling". The objective here is to "optimize an existing solution". There are three steps in this process, which are as follows:
   - Define all limitations and constraints of the problem that needs to be solved.
   - Validation of the linear programming model, in order to ensure that it reflects the business of the situation that it is trying to solve.
   - Solve all of the objective functions, finding the best possible solution. Part of this process also includes examining the constraints and tradeoffs that are involved.

One of the key advantages of linear programming is that it has been around for quite a long time; thus, it is a proven technique. However, it also comes with some disadvantages, which are as follows:

- It is slower and more time-consuming than heuristics. For example, complex problems may take hours to process.
- The model preparation can be very tedious.
- It may be difficult for an inexperienced end user to fully comprehend and understand how the optimization process works in its entirety.

It should be noted at this point that the use of prescriptive analysis comes with its own set of advantages as well as disadvantages. The advantages are as follows:

1. Different Outcomes: The models can create an array of the different possible courses of action that could be taken, as well as their risks.
2. Quicker Responses: When generative AI and machine learning are used, prescriptive modeling can actually work very quickly, and thus, providing insights pinpointed directly at the need.
3. Reduced Errors: When generative AI machine learning are used, the rate of human error is also greatly reduced.

The disadvantages are as follows:

1. Overconfidence: Though generative AI and machine learning being used in prescriptive analytics is still a rather new concept, it is quite possible that the end user could get a little overconfident in the results. The bottom line here is that the computed output is only as accurate as the datasets that are ingested into the model.
2. A Level of Biasness: As just mentioned, if the ingested datasets are not cleansed and optimized beforehand, the output could be greatly skewed. This once again goes back to the phenomenon of "garbage-in and garbage-out", as also examined earlier in this chapter.
3. Algorithms May Be Off: Just as much as the datasets that are ingested, so do the algorithms used in the generative AI and machine learning components in the prescriptive analytics model. If they are not fully optimized on a regular basis, the outputs can be once again be greatly skewed.

The States of Data

So far in this chapter, we have reviewed the following about data:

• The types of data
• The kinds of data models that are available today

It is important to note at this point that data and the corresponding datasets are never static in nature. For example, they are constantly being updated, modified, enhanced, and even deleted if they are deemed to be no longer necessary. In other words, data is always in a dynamic state, especially if generative AI and machine learning are also incorporated into the process, as reviewed throughout this chapter.

So, you may be asking at this point, what are the various activity states of data? They can be described as follows:

- Data in transit
- Data at rest
- Data in use

We will now do a deeper dive into each one of them.

Data in Transit

Just as the name suggests, this refers to when datasets are in "motion" or are in the state of transiting from one point to another, from the point of origination (which would typically be the database in which there are initially stored at) to the point of destination (which would be another server, database, or even a web-based application, a wireless device, etc.). The medium of transit are any forms or types of communications that are digital in nature. This includes the following:

- Email
- Instant collaboration tools like Microsoft Teams, WhatsApp, Zoom, and WebEx.
- Any other type or kind of electronic forum where the datasets can be further accessed

However, whenever data is in transit, it is most vulnerable. There is no true guarantee that the datasets will even reach their final point of destination, and they could even be intercepted by a malicious third party. To help mitigate this risk from happening, businesses often use other options, such as the following:

- Hashing: This is where a specialized algorithm is deployed into the dataset. Essentially, this provides a proof positive to the receiving party (situated at the point of destination) that the datasets have not been altered or manipulated in any way, shape, or form. Typically, the Hashing algorithm consists of a complex set of sequential numbers that are assigned at random. If any of these numbers have not moved, then the receiving party can be assured that the datasets have not been altered. If there is a change in sequence, then that is usually indicative that some alteration of the datasets has occurred along the way.

- Encryption: This is where the datasets are rendered into a garbled, useless state from the point of origination to the point of destination. Thus, if the dataset were to be intercepted by a malicious third party, there is nothing that they can do with it, unless they have the specific key to decrypt it. In these cases, the datasets are encrypted via a public key at the point of origination and are decrypted at the point of destination with the private key.

A public key can be technically defined as follows:

A public key is a large numerical value that is used to encrypt data. The key can be generated by a software program, but more often, it is provided by a trusted, designated authority and made available to everyone through a publicly accessible repository or directory.

*(SOURCE: https://www.techtarget.com/searchsecurity/definition/
public- key#:~:text=In%20cryptography%2C%20a%20public
%20key,publicly%20accessible%20repository %20or%20directory.)*

A private key can be technically defined as follows:

The private key, which is securely stored on the recipient's device, is used to decrypt the data.

*(SOURCE: https://www.preveil.com/blog/public-and-private-
key/#:~:text=Public%20and%20private%20keys%20play,used
%20to%20decrypt%20the%20data.)*

Data at Rest

As its name suggests, these are datasets that are simply archived. Typically, they are stored into a central database, whether it is physical or virtual-based. But it could also mean that it is stored on USB devices, smartphones (primarily those that are iOS and android-based), any other portable storage device, or any type or kind of wireless devices. Data at rest also means that the datasets are by no means in transit from the point of destination to the point of origination.

Data at Rest—Protective Measures

Although the data at rest is deemed to be not nearly as vulnerable as to the data in transit, it is still a prime target for the cyberattacker in terms of data exfiltration and lateral-based attacks. Therefore, the following protective mechanisms are recommended in order to mitigate the risk of this happening:

- The usage of security software
- The implementation of firewalls, whether they are physical or virtual-based. Also consider using the Next Generation Firewall.
- Deploy encryption-based mechanisms.
- Implement the concepts of data loss prevention (this is also known as DLP). These tools are readily available by cloud providers, especially that of Microsoft Azure. But, deploying them for an on premises IT and network infrastructure will prove to be much more difficult to implement.
- Data in Use

As its name suggests, these are the datasets that are being used in some way, shape, or form. It can be both physical and virtual-based. For example, with the former, this will be most common when the end user makes use of datasets at their personal computer or wireless device. For instance, he or should could be editing or modifying data in a database or even an Excel-based spreadsheet. With the latter, it is typically a web-based application that is processing the datasets. Probably one of the best example of this is that of online or E-commerce store. When the customer is ready to make a purchase, he or she will typically enter in their credit card information. From there, the online or E-commerce will then actually process this kind of dataset to complete the transaction.

Another typical example of this is the generative AI or machine learning model. They are always processing datasets, whether it is for training or computing the output to a specific query.

- Data in Use—Protective Measures

  It is at this point that the datasets are deemed to be the most vulnerable. For example, they can also be intercepted by a cyberattacker. Or worst yet, these datasets can be captured from a phishing-based attack. A good example of this was during the COVID-19 pandemic. The cyberattacker would send a cunning phishing Email with a sense of urgency to it, directing the victim to phony site. If the link was clicked, users would be directed to a fictitious website where they would be prompted to enter their username, password, and other financial information such as credit card and banking account numbers.

  To mitigate the risk from this happening, the following protective measures are recommended:

- Make sure that all of your servers (whether physical or virtual-based) are updated with the latest software patches and upgrades.
- Use a password manager that will create and reset long and complex passwords that are difficult to crack.
- Use multifactor authentication (also known as MFA) in order to fully confirm the identity of the end user who is requesting access to the datasets. It is important to note that these authentication mechanisms must be differing in nature. An example of this would be the use of a password, challenge/response question, and RSA token, a biometric modality (such as fingerprint recognition and/or iris recognition), and so on.
- Make sure that your employees are up to par on their levels of "cyber hygiene" by conducting regular security awareness training programs.

  Apart from deploying and implementing the protective measures just described, it is also very important to adopt and implement a set of best practices. These are reviewed in the next three subsections.

- Data in Transit—Best Practices

Here are some recommended best practices for you and your IT security team should follow for data in transit:

1. <u>Create the Groundwork</u>: To achieve this, you should establish solid policies and frameworks that your company needs

to follow. This is one of the best ways to ensure that proper levels of cyber hygiene are being followed, and that nobody is exempt from following them to the letter. Although you can create your baselines in this regard, it is highly recommended that you follow the frameworks that are offered by NIST and CISA. They provide templates on their websites that you can easily download and follow.

2. Implement Automation: Obviously you and your IT security are flooded with tasks on a daily basis, especially when it comes to combating the daily threat variants that are inbound or internal to your business. With this in mind, you should consider automating some of your processes, using the tools of AI. A great example of this is the filtering for false positives. You can use AI and create rules and permutations that filter out for them, thus presenting only the legitimate warnings and alerts to your IT security team. The end benefit of this is that the triaging process will become much more effective and efficient, thus cutting back on the time it takes to respond and contain a threat variant.

3. Make Sure Emails Are Encrypted: The sending and receiving of Email messages still remains the lifeblood of any business, no matter how large or small, or even the industry that it is in. Therefore, you need to make sure that all of your Emails are encrypted, including the attachments, both inbound and outbound. The good news here is that most of the cloud providers, especially that of Microsoft Azure, offer encryption as a default setting in their Email platforms, such as that of Microsoft Exchange.

4. Implement Data Loss Prevention: Although this concept was explored earlier in this chapter, it is still quite important to emphasize its need again. By using "DLP", as it is more commonly known as, you can achieve the following:
   • Avoid the loss of intellectual property, customer data, and other types of PII datasets.
   • Scan for all Emails and their related attachments.
   • Identify and confirm potential vulnerabilities using such items as keywords, file hashes, signature pattern matching, and dictionaries.

- Anything that is deemed to be suspicious can then be quarantined for further review by the IT security team or even sent via a secure content portal, from where the end user can then download whatever they need in a safe manner.
- Data in Use—Best Practices

Here are some recommended best practices for you and your IT security team to follow for data in use:

1. <u>Make Sure Controls Are Deployed</u>: Before you start using any type or kind of datasets, make sure that you have all of the needed controls in place. Determining what is needed in this regard usually first starts out with conducting a Risk Assessment Study, which will allow you to determine and ascertain your most vulnerable assets, both digital and physical. This part is actually imperative, because many of the data privacy laws that are in existence today, such as those of the GDPR, CCPA, HIPAA, and so on, now mandate that these controls have to be put into place.

2. <u>Enforce IAM</u>: This is an acronym that stands for "identity and access management". This is a critical component of your security policies, as it governs who can access what in your business and how those rights, permissions, and privileges are assigned. A crucial area here in this regard is a subfield of IAM that is known as "privileged access management", also known as PAM for short. This area deals with those privileged accounts that have superuser rights, privileges, and permissions that are assigned to them. This is a prime target for the cyberattacker, because if they can get access to these kinds of accounts, they can pretty much gain access to the entire IT and network infrastructure of your business. One of our previously published books, entitled "The Zero Trust Framework and Privileged Access Management (PAM)" covers this much more in detail. More information about this book can be found in the following link:

   https://www.routledge.com/The-Zero-Trust-Framework-and-Privileged-Access-Management-PAM/Das/p/book/9781032742571

3. <u>Managing the Rights</u>: Once again, this falls under the purview of IAM; but when you are assigning the rights, privileges, and permissions to your employees, you need to follow the concept of what is known as "Least Privilege". A technical definition of it is as follows:

> The principle of least privilege (PoLP) refers to an information security concept in which a user is given the minimum levels of access—or permissions—needed to perform his/her job functions. It is widely considered to be a cybersecurity best practice and is a fundamental step in protecting privileged access to high-value data and assets.
>
> *(SOURCE: https://www.cyberark.com/what-is/least-privilege/)*

In simpler terms, you do not want to give out any more rights, privileges, and permission than what is absolutely necessary for your employees to conduct their normal job functions on a daily basis.

• Data in Rest—Best Practices

Here are some recommended best practices for you and your IT security team to follow for data in rest:

1. <u>Implement Full Disk Encryption</u>: Most of the data in rest typically gets stored either in the databases of a server (either physical or virtual) or in the wireless devices of employees. Therefore, it is crucial that all disks (whether physical or virtual) are fully encrypted. In the case of wireless devices, you will also want to make sure that you have the "remote wipe" functionality at hand. So that in case, a wireless device is either lost or stolen. You can issue a simple command that will delete all of the data in the hard drive of the device in question.

2. <u>Deploy a CASB</u>: This is an acronym that stands for "cloud security access broker". A technical definition of it is as follows:

> CASBs combine multiple different security policies, from authentication and credential mapping to encryption, malware detection, and more, offering flexible enterprise solutions that help ensure

cloud app security across authorized and unauthorized applications, and managed and unmanaged devices.

(SOURCE: https://www.microsoft.com/en-us/security/business/
security-101/what-is-a-cloud- access-security-broker-casb)

Put in simple terms, this is another way of deploying DLP solutions, but this time, to your cloud deployment, especially if you have your entire IT and network infrastructure hosted onto it, such as that of Microsoft Azure.

3. Implement an MDVM: This is an acronym that stands for "mobile device management". Simply put, it is a set of security policies that govern how your employees should manage and use their company-issued wireless devices. Two big components of this policy include the following:

   • BYOD: This is an acronym that stands for "bring your own device". This is where employees will use their own personal devices, rather than their company-issued ones.

   • Shadow IT: This is where your employees download and utilize nonauthorized apps onto their company-issued wireless devices. This can pose a huge security risk, and all devices should be monitored and audited on a regular basis to make sure that this does not happen.

The Use of Encryption

A key concept that was highlighted throughout this chapter was that of "encryption". An overview of this was also provided earlier, and because of its sheer importance, it has become a key factor in cybersecurity today. It is important to note that encryption can be very simple to use or it can be quite complex, given the level that your IT and network infrastructure are currently at. Typically, an organization, if large enough, will deploy what is known as a "public key infrastructure", or PKI for short. A technical definition of PKI is as follows:

The Public key infrastructure (PKI) is the set of hardware, software, policies, processes, and procedures required to create, manage, distribute, use, store, and revoke digital certificates and public-keys. PKIs are the foundation that enables the use of technologies, such as digital signatures and encryption, across large user populations.

(SOURCE: https://cpl.thalesgroup.com/faq/public-key-infrastructure-pki/what-public-key-infrastructure-pki)

An image of a PKI is illustrated as follows:

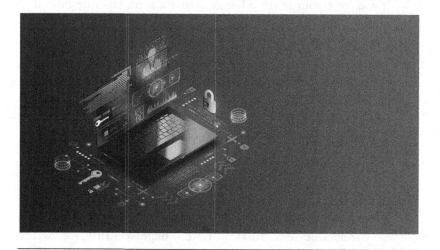

Figure 1.5

(SOURCE: https://www.shutterstock.com/image-illustration/passwordless-authentication-concept-identity-verification-method-2226137889/edit?chatId=6bff1029ef6a429fbcceea99f631d195)

Although it is out of the scope to provide a comprehensive review as to what encryption is all about, a thorough technical review of it can be seen from one of our previous books, entitled *Testing and Securing Web Applications*. It can be viewed at the following link:

https://www.routledge.com/Testing-and-Securing-Web-Applications/Das-Johnson/p/book/9780367333751?utm_source=crcpress.com&utm_medium=referral

Overall, this chapter has provided an extensive overview into what data is all about. It is important to have this understanding, because the rest of this book will now focus on the major data privacy laws. These laws have arisen as a result of the major security breaches that have occurred involving datasets. Their purposes are primarily twofold:

- To give consumers of a business the right to control their PII datasets as they wish.
- To make sure that all appropriate controls are in place to help mitigate the risk of any changes of data exfiltration from happening.

The first major data privacy law that will be covered is that of the GDPR, which is covered in Chapter 2.

Resources

1. https://www.ibm.com/topics/pii
2. https://cloud.google.com/learn/what-is-big-data
3. https://aws.amazon.com/what-is/data-mining
4. https://builtin.com/data-science/multiple-regression
5. https://aws.amazon.com/what-is/monte-carlo-simulation
6. https://careerfoundry.com/en/blog/data-analytics/what-is-random-forest/
7. https://www.javatpoint.com/k-means-clustering-algorithm-in-machine-learning
8. https://www.ibm.com/topics/knn
9. https://www.investopedia.com/terms/a/autoregressive-integrated-moving-average-arima.asp
10. https://www.ibm.com/topics/pii
11. https://www.thoughtspot.com/data-trends/analytics/prescriptive-analytics
12. https://www.techtarget.com/searchsecurity/definition/public-key#:~:text=In%20cryptography%2C%20a%20public%20key,publicly%20accessible%20repository%20or%20directory
13 https://www.preveil.com/blog/public-and-private-key/#:~:text=Public%20and%20private%20keys%20play,used%20to%20decrypt%20the%20data
14. https://www.cyberark.com/what-is/least-privilege
15. https://www.microsoft.com/en-us/security/business/security-101/what-is-a-cloud-access-security-broker-casb
16. https://cpl.thalesgroup.com/faq/public-key-infrastructure-pki/what-public-key-infrastructure-pki

2

AN OVERVIEW OF
THE GDPR

Chapter 1 provided an extensive review into what data is all about. Specifically, there are many kinds and types of them, but in the end, they all belong to two broad categories:

- Quantitative Data: These are datasets that are numerical-based and essentially contain integers of some sort as the primary value in the datasets.
- Qualitative Data: These are datasets which are more subjective in nature. As it was also reviewed in Chapter 1, they can range from being images, videos, audio to SMS-based text messages. While there may be a numerical value attached to them, they are not the core components of these kind of datasets, unlike the quantitative ones.

As it relates to artificial intelligence, it should be noted that the traditional models of machine learning and neural networks work best on quantitative datasets, whereas with generative AI (with the best example of this being ChatGPT), it can ingest both types of datasets and even provide outputs in that format.

The primary reason for providing such an extensive overview into what data is all about is to underscore its sheer importance of what it means to society today, especially for both consumers and businesses. There was a time when threats to these Datasets were just thoughts that occasionally appeared in the back of the mind. But given the interconnectivity and digital nature of datasets today, security breaches have become a real threat.

DOI: 10.1201/9781003496915-2

For example, they are among the most prized target for the cyber-attacker to go after. The primary reason for this is that these are considered to be the proverbial "crown jewels" for any kind of company. Once a cyberattacker has access to these datasets, they can penetrate into just about anything into the IT and network infrastructure, and wreak all kinds of damage to both the customer and the business. In this regard, probably the worst forms of security breaches that can occur are those of ransomware and extortion-like attacks. Another scenario is that the cyberattacker could sell these datasets onto the dark web or even give them to another hacking group that can launch a ransomware attack for literally pennies on the dollar. Technically, this is known as the "ransomware as a service", or RaaS in short.

In response to the recent explosion in these kinds of threats, many of the governments around the world, especially here in the United States and the European Union (EU), have adopted a strict set of laws and regulations that are meant to help protect the datasets that businesses store and further mitigate the risk of them being impacted by a security breach by having the businesses deploy and implement the needed controls in order to make this into a reality. Also, another key objective of these regulations is to give the consumer the option of how they want their own datasets, which is in possession by a company, to be handled.

For example, with these new laws now implemented, the customer of a business can now directly inform them if they want to have their datasets deleted or if they want to have them handled in a different way than previously used, stored, processed, or archived. Also, if a customer becomes a victim of a security breach as a result of a hack that happened at a business where their datasets were stored, the customer has the right to know as to what happened to their particular datasets and what are the course of actions the business has taken to contain and further mitigate the security breach, preventing further impacts. Also, they have the right to ask for an action of recourse, especially when it comes to getting a free credit report and free credit monitoring.

It should be noted at this point that all of these laws and regulation come under the general term of what is known as "data privacy". It can be specifically defined as follows:

Data privacy, also called "information privacy", is the principle that a person should have control over their personal data, including the ability to decide how organizations collect, store and use their data.

(SOURCE: https://www.ibm.com/topics/data-privacy)

So, in order to enforce this particular concept and to fulfill the two-pronged approach described earlier, these regulations have now become known as "data privacy laws". In recent years, there have been a number of them have been formulated, adopted, passed, and implemented. Probably the most famous of these is what is known as the "GDPR", which was set into law by the various countries of the EU.

The "GDPR" is the focal point of the rest of this chapter.

An Overview into the GDPR

GDPR is an acronym that stands for "general data protection regulation". As mentioned previously, this is a data privacy law that was formulated, enacted, and passed by all members of the EU. It has been deemed to be the first of its kind on a global basis, and it is also viewed as one of the most stringent data privacy laws on a global basis. This law came into being officially on May 25, 2018, and because of this history, there is some set of legal precedence that has been set forth to serve as a guidance for future data privacy cases.

When one first thinks of the GDPR, the assumption is that it can have an impact on any one individual and any one business. While this is true on a theoretical basis, there are certain stipulations to this, which are as follows:

- Any business that is subject to the tenets and provisions of the GDPR must first meet a certain revenue size and employee size.
- It is not just businesses and individuals in the EU that can be fully held accountable under the tenets and provisions of the GDPR. It can impact anyone and any business around the world, going on the premise that they have customers and/or offices that are located in the EU. For example, if there is a corporation that is based in California, but has either offices or

customers in the EU, they are subject to the tenets and provisions of the GDPR, assuming that they meet the revenue size and employee size thresholds that have been set forth.

- One of the key provisions of the GDPR is to conduct an audit of any business with ties to the EU. This is not an automatic audit; the main trigger for this is if the business has been impacted by a security breach affecting customer datasets. Even in the absence of a true security breach, any sort of data exfiltration can also trigger an audit. If any of these catalysts does set off an audit, the company is closely scrutinized as to what exactly happened, the steps taken to mitigate and further contain the damage, and the specific procedures implemented to upgrade controls and even deploy new ones to prevent such incidents.

Before we delve further into the GDPR, it is important that you have access to the entire law for your review. In order to view it, access the following link:

http://cyberresources.solutions/Cyber_Compliance_Book/GDPR_
   TEXT.pdf

The Historical Origins of the GDPR

As mentioned previously, although this law was passed in 2016, its origins actually go back much further than that. For example, the first, formal view on what data privacy is actually about came under the auspices of the "European Convention on Human Rights". This came about in 1950, and according to the text back then, data privacy was specifically defined as follows:

Everyone has the right to respect for his private and family life, his home and his correspondence.

(SOURCE: https://www.echr.coe.int/documents/d/echr/Convention_ENG)

Of course back in the 1950s, technology was still very much evolving, and the term "cybersecurity" was not even dreamt of. But as the decades went on, as computing technology advanced and became much powerful in nature, data was starting to be used on a much more frequent and heavy basis. This was especially noted during the early 1990s, which witnessed the growth of the internet era and its corresponding "Dor Com Bubble".

Because business owners and leaders saw data becoming more potentially being at risk, the EU then passed its second forerunner to the GDPR, which became known as the "European Data Protection Directive", also known more formally as the EDPD in short. This piece of legislation was actually passed in 1995, and it established the first set of standards and best practices for the implementation kind of data privacy for consumers of businesses that were based in the EU. However, one of the key caveats of this law was that each country would be responsible for implementing its own version. As a result, this caused all kinds of confusion for businesses; for example, what if a business had offices in both the United Kingdom and France, which set of laws should they abide by? This question would be formally answered by the subsequent passage of the GDPR.

But as the internet continued to proliferate even further, a number of key milestones that were associated were reached. Following are some examples of them:

- The first true online banner appeared on web browsers on a global basis. This can actually be seen in the following link: http://thefirstbannerad.com/
- By the early 2000s, many financial institutions now started to offer various forms of online banking. This gave birth to the web-based version of the traditional brick-and-mortar bank, and, as a result, rather than having to visit one personally, customers could now do everything from the convenience of their home, assuming that they had a solid internet-based connection.
- The first true social media platform, which is now known today as "Facebook", was officially launched.
- In 2011, the first major lawsuit regarding suspicious online activity was filed. It was a user of Google that filed this, making claims that this platform illegally and covertly scanned their Email messages.

Because of all these events that were transpiring, both business leaders and political leaders quickly saw the need to formulate and set into motion a common set of best practices and standards that would serve as one uniform law for all the countries that were part of the EU. But rather than coming up with something from scratch, the business leaders and the political leaders decided instead to use the "EDPD" as the basis for what would now become known as the GDPR. The primary driver was simple objective, which is as follows:

A comprehensive approach on personal data protection.

(SOURCE: https://gdpr.eu/what-is-gdpr/)

As described earlier in this section, the GDPR became formal law on May 25, 2018, but members of the EU already started to informally adopt its key provisions and tenets even as early as 2016. It is important to note at this point that a key difference between the GDPR and previous legislations that were passed is that this law set one common set of rules that all member countries must follow. The main benefit of this is that there is much less confusion as to the kind of law that needs a business needs to come in compliance with.

Referring back to our example of a corporation with offices in both the United Kingdom and France, which transacts business in both countries, before the advent of the GDPR, this particular corporation would have had to abide by two different set of laws. But under the provisions and tenets of the GDPR, this corporation now has to comply with just one set of laws.

It should also be noted at this point that the GDPR is also the forerunner of many data privacy laws that are now coming to force in the United States. The primary example of this is the "California Consumer Privacy Act", also known as "CCPA". This can be considered as a "mini version" of the GDPR, as it only regulates organizations that transact business in the state of California or have customers there. But unlike the GDPR, the United States, at the present time, does not have just one law that regulates data privacy, rather, all fifty states are creating their own version of law, which is creating all sorts of confusion. For example, if an entity transacts business in all fifty states, which data privacy law takes precedence over the others? This is a question that has yet to be formally answered today.

The events leading to the birth of the formal GDPR is illustrated in Figure 2.1.

Figure 2.1 A History of the Data Privacy Laws

Key Concepts of the GDPR

Now that we have provided an extensive history in the background of the GDPR, the next few sections of this chapter examine the major components and concepts that are associated with. There is no doubt that the GDPR is a voluminous, rather large, and complex piece of legislation. In fact, there are even experts and specialists who specialize in this and make this their entire profession. In fact, there is also a related subject to the GDPR that is called the "CMMC". It is an acronym that stands for the "Cybersecurity Maturity Model Certification".

This is where the Department of Defense (DoD) of the Federal Government requires defense contractors and their related subcontractors to come into a certain level of compliance before they are allowed to bid on contracts or even complete a project that they are currently working on. This requirement ensures that these entities have the appropriate controls in place to safeguard the confidential and private information and data that both the DoD and the Federal Government are entrusting them with. While the provisions and tenets will not be exactly the same as the GDPR, the central theme still surrounds itself around on the theme of data privacy. In fact, the CMMC is a topic that will be explored and reviewed in more detail later in this book.

But in terms of the GDPR in this chapter, it would be out of the scope of this book to cover each and every aspect of it. Therefore, we will cover the major parts of it, so that you can take relevant aspects of it and apply it fortifying the controls that you have in place at your business to protect your datasets, where ever they are stored at, whether it is in a physical or virtual device or even a physical database that is stored on premises or a virtual database that is provisioned in the cloud, such as that of Microsoft Azure.

So in this effort, here are the underlying concepts that you as the CISO and your IT security team need to fully understand. They are as follows:

1. The Personal Data: This can be technically defined as follows:

> Personal data is any information that relates to an individual who can be directly or indirectly identified. Names and email addresses are obviously personal data.

> *(SOURCE: https://gdpr.eu/what–is–gdpr/)*

In other words, personal data are those distinguishable factors that confirm the identity of a particular individual. It is important to note that these factors can be both physical and digital in nature, and examples of these are as follows:

- Geo location–based information and data
- The ethnicity of the individual
- The gender of the individual
- Websites that have been accessed by the individual
- Any sort of web cookies that have been left on the device of the end user (it is important to note here that it is primarily because of the GDPR that a majority of the websites today have to offer the end user the choice of whether to accept or decline the use of cookies).
- Any social media sites that the end user has a distinct and complete profile on.

2. The Data Processing: This can be technically defined as follows:

Any action performed on data, whether automated or manual.

(SOURCE: https://gdpr.eu/what-is-gdpr/)

Although this is a very broad definition and has very broad applications, probably of the simplest examples of this is when an end user submits a financial transaction at a website, such as an online store in order purchase products and/or services from the online merchant. It should be noted that the actual credit card or banking information cannot be stored, the buying and purchasing history of the customer can be stored, as well as the various areas of the website that they have visited. But of course, the online merchant has to notify ahead of time the end user of the types of information and data that they are collecting in this regard. Another example of this is when the end user visits the website of for instance, that of a cybersecurity vendor and fills out the proverbial "Contact Us" page. All of the information and data that get submitted are also used in varying degrees to identify the end user; but before they are actually allowed to submit this, they have to consent to this, by usually checking a box toward the bottom of the "Contact Us" page.

3. <u>The Data Subject</u>: This can be technically defined as follows: The person whose data is processed.

In other words, this is the person who is submitting their information and data for later use by the business. Once again, a prime example of this is the end user submitting both their personal and financial information and data at online store.

4. <u>The Data Controller</u>: This can be technically defined as follows:

> The person who decides why and how personal data will be processed.

> *(SOURCE: https://gdpr.eu/what-is-gdpr/)*

As this relates to the IT security team, it could very well be a designated person in that area who decides how all of the information and data that are collected will actually be processed. In the end, it should not be anybody else that decides this, because along with the processing of the data and information, the appropriate controls also have to be put into place, and truthfully, it is only the members of the IT security team that can do this the best. Also, it is quite possible that the business may even hire out a "virtual-based chief compliance officer" to this is task, who would be ultimately hired on a contract basis.

5. <u>The Data Processor</u>: This can be technically defined as follows:

> A third party that processes personal data on behalf of a data controller.

> *(SOURCE: https://gdpr.eu/what-is-gdpr/)*

The preferred way would be to have a business to this process as an internal function. But given the uptick in digital demand, many organizations are now contracting this out to "third-party suppliers" to accomplish this task. Although there may be cost-savings associated with this, it can also be a huge security risk. Therefore, if a business were to choose this kind of option, they have to carefully vet out any third-party suppliers before ultimately deciding on one.

The Key Tenets of the GDPR

Although the GDPR is very picky and very enforceable for all stages of the dataset process (as reviewed in Chapter 1), the legislation is extremely particular about how the datasets are actually processed. The primary reason for this is that the stage where the datasets are the most vulnerable and the most prone to a security breach. They are especially vulnerable if you and your IT security team have outsourced this particular function to a third-party supplier.

For example, even though the representatives of the third-party supplier may have signed and executed all of the agreements, there is still the grave risk that there could be a weakening or vulnerability in their own IT and network infrastructure, or even worst yet, the datasets that you have trusted them with could be prone to an insider attack, which are often very difficult to detect until it is too late. So, in a huge effort to counter all of this and to make sure that the appropriate controls are in place and fully optimized, there are a total of seven "protection and accountability principles" that any business must fully adhere to if they fall under the tenets and provisions of the GDPR, provided that they met both the revenue size and employee size.

These guiding principles are as follows:

1. Accountability: The purpose of this principle is to make the business aware that they will be held to the fullest levels of responsibility in the protection of all of the datasets, whether it is the customer or even their own employees. And, should a security breach occur to them or there is an incident of data exfiltration, the degree of responsibility will be even greater. This will even subject the business to an extensive audit and will even face harsh financial penalties. This aspect of the GDPR will be reviewed later in this chapter. But for this principle, the following are the tenets and provisions:
   • Each and every member of the IT security, third-party supplier, and so on must be designated their own levels of responsibility. Their duties have to be carefully detailed to them, and they have to be informed of the consequences as well if they fail to live up to the expectations that are required of them.
   • At each and every step of the dataset processing chain, it must be thoroughly documented. In this regard, particular emphasis has to be paid to how the datasets are

stored, where they are being stored, and the exact steps and nature of how they will be processed. Even a schedule of when the controls were deployed and upgraded has to be included in this documentation as well.

- Security awareness training must be given to all of those employees who are entrusted in handling the datasets. They must be taught the proper procedures in how to handle them and the steps that need to be taken in triaging if a security breach were to actually happen.

- Especially when third-party suppliers are processing the datasets that you have entrusted them with, you must have them sign and execute detailed contracts of all the dataset handling procedures and the level of responsibility that they are fully expected to abide by.

- If at all possible and feasible, the business must also employ a dedicated "data protection officer", also known as DPO in short. This job title can be technically defined as follows:

The purpose of the General Data Protection Regulation (GDPR) is to safeguard personal data on the Internet. To this end, the GDPR requires most organizations that handle people's private information to appoint an employee charged with overseeing the organization's GDPR compliance. The Data Protection Officer, or DPO, is an organization's GDPR focal point and will have to possess expert knowledge of data protection law and practices.

(SOURCE: https://gdpr.eu/data-protection-officer/)

In this regard, the DPO has the following roles to fulfill in order to make sure that all parties involved are in lock-step, ensuring that the datasets are being processed with the utmost levels of security in mind:

*Address and answer all questions and/or concerns that the customer may have to how their particular datasets are being handled.

*To keep informed all stakeholders who are involved in the dataset processing phase of their responsibilities on a regular basis.

*Have the ability to perform compliance audits on a regular basis to make sure that the controls that are associated with the datasets are fully optimized.

*In conjunction with the IT security team, conduct regular vulnerability assessments on the datasets to make sure that any weaknesses or gaps that are discovered are completely remediated.

*In the case of an audit, the DPO must be able to cooperate with the investigative authorities and produce any sort of documentation or evidence that is requested in a prompt and timely manner.

*The DPO will be and act accordingly as the "supervisory authority" on all compliance issues as it relates and pertains to the datasets that are stored, in transit, or archived.

2. The Data Security: As the name of this principle highly suggests, this is a task that should be primarily left to the CISO and their corresponding IT security team. After all, they will have all of the tools, training, and know-how in order to make sure that the right controls have been deployed in order to protect the datasets. Also, they will know how to diagnose any gaps or vulnerabilities that have been found, which can be accomplished through either penetration testing or threat hunting, or perhaps even a combination of both. In other words, their main duties to the datasets is defined as follows:

Implementing appropriate technical and organizational measures.

(SOURCE: https://gdpr.eu/what-is-gdpr/)

Although the above definition is quite broad in scope and nature, the following are examples of how it can be done:

- Deploying Multifactor Authentication, also known as MFA in short: As it has been reviewed earlier in this book, this refers to the fact that at least three or more differing authentication mechanisms are being used to fully ascertain and confirm the identity of an individual who is involved the processing of the datasets.

- **Making use of a password manager:** For example, passwords have always been a nemesis to the IT security team, as this is probably one of the most prized possessions for the cyberattacker. But end users often use weak passwords so that they are easy to remember or even use the same ones over and over again. But with the password manager, very long and complex passwords can be created, which are thus, very difficult to crack. Another key benefit of using the password manager is that it can establish and reset new passwords on a regular schedule that you create for it.

- **Making the use of encryption:** This is a concept that was also reviewed in Chapter 1. Essentially, this is where you and your IT security team scramble the datasets into a garbled format, starting from the point of origination to the point of destination. That way, if the datasets were to be intercepted by a malicious third party, there is nothing that they can really do with them unless they have the appropriate private key to unscramble the datasets.

- **Deploying a strong IAM policy:** As it was also reviewed in Chapter 1, this is an acronym that stands for "identity and access management". This is an area of cybersecurity that governs how the rights, privileges, and permissions for each entity and/or end user will be assigned if they are working in the processing stages of the datasets. It is very important in this regard to implement the concept of "least privilege", which was also reviewed earlier in this book.

- **Implement a data privacy policy:** Along with your security policies, your business should also really have a data privacy policy in place to go along with it. It can be technically defined as follows:

A privacy policy is a legal document that explains how an organization handles any customer, client or employee information gathered in its operations. It will include how data is collected, stored, used, shared and protected and the user's rights in connection to the data.

(SOURCE: https://www.techtarget.com/whatis/definition/privacy-policy)

This is not an option, in fact, having a data privacy policy is now a mandated requirement across all countries that are in the EU, the state of California (because of the CCPA), and other states that have a data privacy law that is either introduced as a bill or is expected to pass votes so that it will become an actual law.

3. The protection of the datasets: Although this book so far has examined on a broad level the technical ways in which the datasets should be protected, the GDPR has yet another view on this. For example, the protection of datasets should be ingrained "by design and default" into the development of any new product or service that your business may come up with. This simply means that along with the engineering aspect, you also need to include how the datasets will be collected, stored, archived, and used once launched to new customers and prospects. Apart from this aspect, the GDPR requires you to consider the safeguards and controls that will be deployed throughout every step in the research and development phases to make sure that the datasets are protected to the maximum extent possible.

4. The Consent: This is probably one of the most "sacred" components of the GDPR, as it relates to the end user. The GDPR clearly stipulates that datasets can only be collected from a customer unless they have their clear and explicit permission to do so. Depending on the type of the data that is being collected, written permission may be required; but for the most part, if a customer or prospect simply visits a website or consents to having their information being submitted on the "Contact Us", that is also usually good enough. But despite this, there are five key provisions and tenets that the business must abide to in this regard. They are as follows:

   • The permission that is provided by the customer or prospect must be as follows:

   freely given, specific, informed and unambiguous.

   (SOURCE: https://gdpr.eu/what-is-gdpr/)

   • All permissions must be in clear and easy-to-understand language.

- The customer or prospect of the business can withdraw their particular right to consent at any time they wish to, but the caveat here is that it must be provided in writing.
- Any child under the age of 13 cannot provide the right to consent on their own, rather they must also have the written and explicit of their parents or legal guardian.
- All evidence of the right to consent must be thoroughly documented by the business and must be provided on demand by a regulatory agent of the GDPR.

5. The Data Protection Officer: Although one of the previous principles just reviewed stated that the appointment of a DPO is highly recommended, there are three specific instances where one will be required. These are as follows:

- The entity is a public serving one, such as that of a state or local government agency.
- Your main business processes require that you keep a constant eye on the activity of your customers. In this regard, some good examples of this are Internet Service Providers (ISPs), Cloud Service Providers (CSPs), Managed Service Providers (MSPs), and Managed Security Service Providers (MSSPs).
- Your business is heavily involved in that of the wide-scale processing of datasets under certain categories. This will fall under "Article 9" of the GDPR. Or, if your business involves the processing of datasets that are associated with individuals who are convicted of a crime and are currently serving time in a penal institution, this will fall under "Article 10" of the GDPR.

But, the bottom line with this principle is that it is always best to have a DPO at all times, especially if your business comes under audit by regulators of the GDPR.

6. Customer/Prospect Rights: One of the most critical aspects of the GDPR is the rights that it spells out, which each customer and prospect has with regard to their datasets. These rights are as follows:

- Informed: The customer/prospect has the right to be told in clear and simple terms what is going on with their datasets. They have the right to ask this at any point in time, and in turn the business must provide a written response within at least two to three business days.

- Access: The customer/prospect has the right to access their datasets on a real-time basis and whenever they wish to do this.
- Rectification: If the customer/prospect sees any omissions, gaps, or other flaws and errors in their datasets, the business must correct or "rectify" this situation within two or three business days.
- Erasure: The customer/prospect has the right to have their datasets removed from the business at any point in time that they wish to, but this must be provided in writing first.
- Restrictions: The customer/prospect has the right to know how their datasets are being processed. If they are not comfortable with how this is proceeding, they have the right to put any restrictions they want at any point in time. But once again, this must be provided in writing to the business.
- Portability: The customer/prospect has the right to know how their datasets are being transferred from one medium to another. For example, they have the right to know if their datasets have been moved from on-premises databases to a virtual database in the cloud, such as Microsoft Azure. Also, they have the sheer right to know if any third-party supplier has access to or is processing their datasets.
- Objections: The customer/prospect has the right to object as to how their datasets are being specifically used. If the business cannot provide an appropriate response, the customer/prospect has the right to obtain legal counsel to get to the bottom of the matter.
- Automation: The customer/prospect has the right to know if their datasets are being processed by an automated tool, namely that of artificial intelligence and generative AI. If the customer/prospect objects to this, the business must immediately cease to process their particular datasets in this particular fashion.

7. <u>Data Processing</u>: As a business, the first instinct is to process the datasets you receive on a timely basis. In other words, you want to examine and analyze it so that you can glean information to better serve your customers. More importantly, this will give you the edge to stay ahead of the competition. While this process can be done almost instantaneously, the GDPR stipulates certain provisions and tenets that your business must follow before you can actually engage in this activity. These are as follows:

- <u>Consent</u>: If you are processing the datasets of your customers and prospects, you must have their written and explicit consent to do this first. If you don't follow this, your business could be subject to a heavily scrutinized audit by the GDPR regulators.

- <u>Contracts</u>: If you need to process the datasets prior to entering a mandatory contract or agreement, this is allowed. A good example of this is processing a loan application from a customer. Of course, you will need to run the appropriate background checks and credit/financial checks before an actual loan can be approved. But even before doing this, you still need to have the written consent of the customer to carry out this particular activity.

- <u>Legalities</u>: If you are required to process datasets from a legal authority (such as a Court of Law), you will have no choice but to do this. But in this case, the Court of Law is actually giving you the consent to do this.

- <u>Emergencies</u>: If the life of an individual is in jeopardy and if datasets have to be processed to save the life of this particular individual, this is allowed without any explicit consent. A prime example of this is the emergency room of a hospital. If a patient is brought in with life-threatening conditions, then by all means, their datasets will have to be processed by medical professionals to deliver the right kinds and dosages of the needed medications.

- <u>Public Interest</u>: If your business is involved in serving public services, explicit consent will not be required beforehand. For example, if a law enforcement official needs to apprehend a suspect, they will need their datasets to be processed in order for this to happen, whether they have the cooperation of the individual or not.

- Legitimate Interest: If you firmly believe that your business has a good enough reason to process the datasets of a customer that will serve their business interests, you can process their datasets without explicit consent to serve this particular purpose. But this can be very subjective, and the first priority here is to serve the "fundamental rights and freedoms of the data subject".

These principles are illustrated in Figure 2.2.

The Penalties of the GDPR

If your business does not abide by or come into compliance with the various tenets and provisions of the GDPR, as they have been reviewed so far in this chapter, your organization could be the subject of a very extensive audit and can even face very harsh penalties.

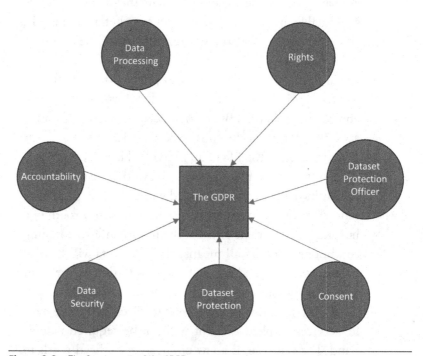

Figure 2.2   The Components of the GDPR

This is obviously a situation that you do not want to face. For example, and audit can take many months to complete, depending on the nature of the violation that you are facing; but apart from the fines imposed, this whole process can also be very costly to your bottom line, especially where the legal expenses are concerned.

But despite this, many businesses still fail to fully understand and comprehend what the breakdowns of the fines and penalties truly are. In this section, we take a closer look at this.

The Monetary Fines

There are two specific tiers or levels of financial penalties that can be imposed by the regulatory bodies that are tasked with enforcing the GDPR. They are as follows:

1. The Lesser Financial Penalty: In this kind of scenario, the financial penalties can be one or both of the following:
   - A fine of up to 10 million euros, or approximately 10,647,088.935 US dollars
   - 2% of the gross revenue of the business in the previous year

   In most cases, only one or the other penalty will be imposed. It is only in severe cases that both financial penalties can be imposed. The following are examples of infractions at this level:
   - Any violations in the collection and processing steps of the datasets would involve the controllers and the entities that process the datasets, whether it is done internally or outsourced to a third-party supplier, as reviewed throughout this book.
   - Any bias or favoritism that has taken place in evaluations and assessments used to gauge the effectiveness and optimization level of controls to protect the datasets would involve the certification bodies that conduct and execute these kinds of exercises.
   - Any violations in the procedures involved in reporting infringements or violations against the provisions and tenets of the GDPR would involve the monitoring bodies and agencies tasked with this responsibility.

2. <u>The Higher Financial Penalty</u>: In this kind of scenario, the financial penalties can be one or both of the following:

- A fine of up to 20 million euros, or 21,287,171.393 US dollars
- 2% of the gross revenue of the business in the previous year

In most cases, only one or the other penalty will be imposed. It is only in severe cases that both financial penalties can be imposed. The following are examples of infractions at this level:

- According to the GDPR, the processing of the datasets must be done as follows:

  Data processing must be done in a lawful, fair, and transparent manner. It has to be collected and processed for a specific purpose, be kept accurate and up to date, and processed in a manner that ensures its security.

  (SOURCE: https://gdpr.eu/fines/)

  In another words, if there is a clear and distinct violation of any of the principles that have taken place (as reviewed in the last section), the business will be subject to a very extensive and exhaustive audit. As stated earlier in this chapter, this is the one area that the regulatory bodies that enforce the GDPR take ***extremely seriously***.

- There is no existing documentation on hand to prove that a customer has given explicit and written consent to have their datasets processed.

- If the prospect and/or customer has not been given any kind or type of written notification as to how the business is using and processing their datasets. Also, if any requests by the prospect and/or customer to have a copy of their datasets, or to have them corrected, deleted, or transferred to another source, are not responded to by the business and are totally ignored, it is considered to be a very serious violation of the GDPR.

- If any of the datasets have been transferred to a different office of the business in a completely different country that has not been approved by the GDPR is also considered to be a very serious violation. In this regard, the issue of dataset storage and processing becomes very murky if it is contained in a cloud-based deployment, such as that of the AWS or Microsoft Azure. For example, although the business may have set up their cloud subscription in approved nation, as determined by the GDPR, there is also the chance that the datasets could be residing in a virtual server or virtual database in a nonapproved country, as just described. The primary reason for this happening is that the cloud service providers have many data centers that are located in many different countries or they could outsource their processed to yet another cloud provider. For example, if the business has requested that the virtual server or virtual database be stored in a data center that is physically located in the country in which their headquarters are located, the virtualization of them could be done by a different third-party supplier.

It is important to note at this point that the GDPR also allows for the member EU nations to, within a certain extent, even create some sub laws, which are derivatives of the major tenets and provisions detailed in this chapter. But these have to be approved by a regulatory body that enforces the GDPR, and if it has not been yet approved and the sub laws are enacted, this is a clear violation of the GDPR.

Finally, if a business refused to comply with any orders that have been given by a regulatory body, this is yet another clear violation of the GDPR. In this case, there will be no audit or chance of appeal, and the harshest financial penalty will be imposed as a result.

Determining the Financial Penalty

It is important to note that when the regulatory agents that enforce the tenets and provisions of the GDPR levy a fine against a business, it is not simply a "flat fee" unless it is a certain percentage of revenue, as reviewed in the last subsection. Instead, certain factors need to be taken into consideration in order to determine the exact fine that is to be imposed. They are as follows:

1. <u>The Nature</u>: There are certain key questions that need to be asked and answered. They are as follows:
   - What was the exact nature of the infringement?
   - How did the infringement exactly happen?
   - Why did the infringement happen
   - How many people were actually affected by the infringement?
   - What was the exact damage that they suffered from, as a result of the infringement?
   - How long did it take to actually detect and respond to the infringement?

   The aforementioned are just the base questions, and, of course, other questions will most likely be asked as well, depending on what exactly happened.

2. <u>The Intention</u>: This part will actually delve into why the infringement actually happened in the first place. For example, was it purely out of negligence or was it malicious in nature?

3. <u>The Mitigation</u>: In this part, it is important to ascertain the exact steps that were taken to contain the effects of the infringement. If it relates to a cybersecurity issue, the key metric here to use would be the "mean time to respond", or the "MTTR", as reviewed throughout this book.

4. <u>The Safeguards</u>: In this regard, it is important to note what exact controls were in place when the infringement actually happened. Some key questions to ask here include the following:
   - Were the controls adequate enough in the first place to have prevented the infringement?
   - Was a schedule put in place by the CISO and IT security team to make sure that the controls were fully optimized at all times?
   - Was the aforementioned schedule fully adhered to or were there any gaps that are present?
   - What is the plan of action now to further improve and/ or replace the existing controls so that the same kind and type of infringement never happens again?

5. <u>The History</u>: Does the business in question have a past history of repeated violations against the tenets and provisions of the GDPR? Or for that matter, do any previous violations exist

with other data privacy laws that the business must adhere to, such as the CCPA, HIPAA, etc.?

6. The Cooperation: In this regard, it will need to be determined if the relevant parties that are associated with the infringement. Some key questions to ask here include the following:
   - Were all of the evidentiary documents produced on time, as requested?
   - How open were the related parties in terms of answering any questions?
   - How open were the related parties when new suggestions and recommendations were imparted to them by the regulatory agents of the GDPR?
   - Were there any attempts of deceive or not telling the truth about the details of the infringement to the regulatory agents of the GDPR?

7. The Data: This is probably by far one of the most important areas in the investigation of the infringement. Some key questions to ask here include the following:
   - What were the datasets that were impacted?
   - What function did they serve in business?
   - How much of the database was actually impacted?
   - How were these datasets impacted? Was it the cause of a cyberattack, data exfiltration, or an insider attack?
   - What kind of corrective and/or mitigative efforts were offered to the impacted key stakeholders if their datasets were compromised as a result of the infringement?
   - Was a risk assessment study initially conducted of the database to determine if it possessed any gaps or weaknesses?
   - What remediative actions were taken to correct these gaps and weaknesses, if any were done at all?

8. The Notification: In this regard, some of the key questions to ask here include the following:
   - How quickly were the key stakeholders notified if their datasets were impacted by an infringement?
   - How were they notified? Was it done by Email, postal mail, phone call, social media post, or others?
   - What kinds of corrective and/or mitigative actions were offered by the business to the key stakeholders that were impacted by the infringement? For example, if it was a

customer, were they offered free credit monitoring, as well as a copy of their credit report on a regular basis?

- Is there an established "hotline" in place so that the key stakeholders can call in or send an Email (or even both) on a real-time basis in order to have their concerns and/or questions answered?
- How quick was the CISO and IT security team in responding to the above queries?

9. The Certifications: Depending on the particular line of business the organization is in and the kind or type of industry that they serve, the entity may have to be certified by other regulatory bodies as well. So in this regard, some of the key questions to ask here include the following:
- What were the certifications?
- What are the nature and scope of these certifications?
- Did the business in question keep these certifications up-to-date and active? Were there any lapses in this, and, if so, what were they? Were any remediative actions taken?
- Did the business in question follow the practices and mandates that were required by these certifications?
- If there were any lapses to the above, how were they remediated, if they were at all?

10. Other Factors: In this regard, the regulatory agents of the GDPR would want to know if there were any other extraneous impacts that may have occurred as a result of the infringement. Some key questions to ask here include the following:
- Were there other stakeholders that were indirectly impacted by the infringement?
- If so, how were they notified?
- Were they given any type or kind of remediative and/or corrective offerings?
- Were there other parts of the business that were indirectly impacted a result of the infringement?
- What were the other financial ramifications of the infringement? For example, what was the financial impact due to:
  *Any downtime that was experienced if the infringement led to an actual security breach.

*If the business had the proper incident response, disaster recovery, and business plans in place.

*If so, were they followed and rehearsed/practiced on a regular basis?

*What were the other financial impacts as a result of the infringement? Examples include brand/reputation loss, loss of customers, etc.

*Were there any lawsuits filed against the business by the key stakeholders as a result of the infringement?

The aforementioned are the key questions that will need to be addressed by the regulatory agencies, but, of course, many more will need to be asked depending on the nature and severity of the infringement in question. It is also very important to keep in mind that it could very well take a long period of time until a final financial penalty can be calculated and assessed, because of all of the variables, such as the ones reviewed, that need to be taken into consideration.

The Impacts of the GDPR on Remote Work

The concept and practice of remote work has been around for a long time, but the recent COVID-19 pandemic made the notion of a 99% remote workforce into a reality. It was originally forecasted that this would happen later this decade, but we are seeing it happen now. The COVID-19 pandemic taught us many lessons, especially key issues on the cybersecurity front. Some of these are as follows:

- The risks that are associated with the intermeshing of both the business and home networks.
- The risks have been brought up due to video conferencing, such as using Zoom, WebEx, and Microsoft Teams.
- The weaknesses that have been brought up with network security tools, especially those like the Virtual Private Network (also known as the VPN). Although this tool was designed to handle a remote workforce, it has not been designed to meet the bandwidth and connectivity needs of a nearly 99% of the workforce. Because of this, many vulnerabilities associated with the VPN have been exposed, thus making it a prime target for cyberattackers.

- The drastic rise in generative AI-borne phishing Emails.
- The explosion in the creation of phony and fictitious websites.
- The rise in social engineering attacks, especially where generative AI is now being used to create deep fakes, in order to make a fictitiously created persona look like a real and legitimate human being.

But the one area of concern of the GDPR is the transmission of datasets from a remote device to the business servers, and vice versa. This risk has heighted greatly due to the fact that many employees have used their personal device in which to conduct their daily job tasks. This is also known as "bring your own device", also known as BYOD in short. Although the GDPR has no specific framework to address the cybersecurity issues that are related to remote work, it suggests following the framework that is provided by the NIST, which is as follows:

1. Identification: The business must correctly identify and fully understand the cyber threat landscape that they are facing. Once again, this can be done by conducting an exhaustive risk assessment study and using all log files that have been outputted from the network security devices in order to predict what the future threat variants could look like. This is an area in which generative AI can be used to help automate this process and to make more accurate predictions.
2. Protection: In this regard, the appropriate controls must be put in place to mitigate the risks of a security breach from impacting both the digital assets and the physical assets. These controls need to be monitored on a $24 \times 7 \times 365$ basis and will need to be either replaced in its entirety or upgraded as needed.
3. Detection: This is how quickly the CISO and the IT security team can actually ascertain if a security breach is underway. The most appropriate metric here would be the "mean time to detect", or MTTD in short. Some of the best exercises that can be deployed here in this regard are those of penetration testing and threat hunting.
4. Response: This refers to how quickly the CISO and their IT security team can actually respond to a security breach, and

actually contain it. The most appropriate metric here would be the "mean time to detect", or MTTD in short. In this regard, having a comprehensive incident response plan becomes very crucial.

5. Recovery: This refers to how quickly the CISO and their IT security team can bring back mission critical operations in the shortest amount of time possible, and eventually bring the business back to the state where it was before the security breach actually happened. In this regard, having a comprehensive disaster recovery and business continuity plans become of grave importance.

It is important to note at this point that the GDPR also makes strong usage of what is known as the "CIA model of cybersecurity". CIA is an acronym that stands for confidentiality, integrity, and availability. The main emphasis this model is on the datasets that a business possesses. These terms can be technically defined as follows:

- Confidentiality:

    Confidentiality involves protecting sensitive data private and safe from unauthorized access.

    (SOURCE: https://www.coursera.org/articles/cia-triad)

- Integrity:

    Data integrity is important to make sure data … are accessing accurate information.

    (SOURCE: https://www.coursera.org/articles/cia-triad)

- Availability:

    Availability refers to the idea that the people who need access to data can get it—without affecting its confidentiality or integrity.

    (SOURCE: https://www.coursera.org/articles/cia-triad)

The "CIA model" is illustrated in Figure 2.3.

As you can see from the illustration, all of these concepts are interrelated with one another.

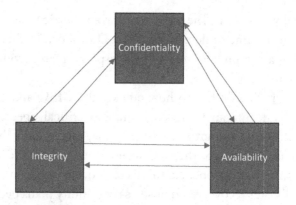

Figure 2.3 The CIA Triad

The Impacts of the GDPR on the Data at Rest and Data in Transit

The GDPR is also very strict when it comes to the datasets that are both at rest and in transit. Although it was reviewed in extensive detail in the last chapter, it is important to provide a brief summary as to what they are again:

1. <u>Data in Transit</u>: These are the datasets that are in transition from the point of origin to the point of destination. The most common instance of this is when an employee of a business requests access to the shared server, and in turn is given the resources that they are looking for. This is illustrated in Figure 2.4.

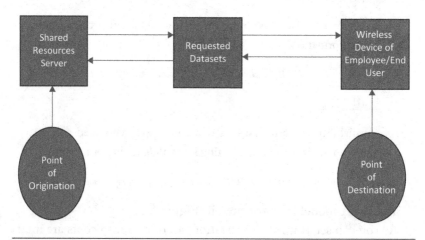

Figure 2.4 Requesting Access to Shared Resources

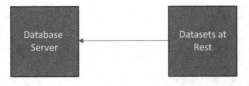

Figure 2.5   Datasets at Rest

2. <u>Data at Rest</u>: In this instance, the datasets remain in a "hiber-nated" state until they are needed again. This is illustrated in Figure 2.5.

When it comes to the GDPR, it is "Recital 83" that clearly stipu-lates that the needed controls have to be deployed for both of these kinds of datasets and that they should be monitored for any gaps or vulnerabilities that may come up on a 24 × 7 × 365 basis. Further, any upgrades and/or remediation must be done on a rapid basis in order to mitigate the risks of any data exfiltration from occurring.

Also, as "Recital 32" of the GDPR also stipulates, and encryp-tion and access control must be implemented as well. As it was also reviewed in the last chapter, encryption is the process of scrambling the datasets into a garbled state that is totally useless, in case if it were to be intercepted by a malicious third party. The only way that the datasets can be rendered back into a useful and comprehensible state is if a private key is used.

In terms of this, the GDPR also requires that encryption must be deployed and implemented across all major technological platforms, which include the following:

- Windows 10 and Windows 11
- iOS-based devices
- Android-based devices
- macOS-based devices
- Linux-based devices

The GDPR also mandates that the concept of "least privilege" must also be used in when assigning the rights, permissions, and privileges to each and every employee who will need to access the datasets. This concept states no more than what is absolutely necessary should be given out in order for the employees to conduct their daily job tasks and assignments.

Figure 2.6

(SOURCE: https://www.shutterstock.com/image-photo/vpn-virtual-private-network-security-encrypted-1141357184)

Also, the GDPR strongly urges of the use of what is known as a "virtual private network", also known as a VPN in short, especially when remote employees have to access the datasets. Essentially, a VPN provides a "secret tunnel" of sorts so that no information and data can be intercepted by a malicious third party. This is especially critical for the datasets in transit. An example of a VPN is illustrated below:

The Impacts of the GDPR Web-Based "Cookies"

Another area where the GDPR pays very close attention is related to the "cookies" that your web browser, whether it is Microsoft Edge, Google Chrome, Mozilla Firefox, Apple Safari, and so on. While most of us have heard of the concept of a "cookie", it is also very important to understand the technical definition of it. It is as follows:

Cookies (often known as internet cookies) are text files with small pieces of data—like a username and password—that are used to identify your computer as you use a network. Specific cookies are used to identify specific users and improve their web browsing experience. Data stored in a cookie is created by the server upon your connection.

(SOURCE: https://usa.kaspersky.com/resource-center/definitions/cookies)

As you can see from the definition, while the amount of information that the cookie actually collect is quite small, over time, it can be built up, and, as a result, a profile about you can be built and created by the website(s) that you are visiting. Because of this, this is also considered to be an area of data privacy by the GDPR. In the past, an end user would never receive any kind of notification that their web browser was being deployed with cookies.

But with close eyes by the GDPR on this, you will notice that many websites provide a notification that your web browsing history will be making the use of cookies. From here, you are then given a choice if you would like to continue or not. In some cases, you will still even have the option to outright reject the use of the cookies on that particular website, and you can still continue to use it. But, some of the functionalities of that particular website may not be usable, until you accept the use of cookies.

In this regard, the GDPR recognizes three categories of cookies that fall under its purview. They are as follows:

1. The Duration: The cookies in this category are as follows:
   - Session Cookies: These are actually temporary in nature and are only active once you go into website and become deactivated once you close that website.
   - Persistent Cookies: Although these kinds of cookies have a finite lifespan and do expire, they reside permanently on your hard drive until you delete them out completely.
2. The Provenance: The cookies in this category are as follows:
   - First-Party Cookies: When you first visit a particular website, these kinds of cookies are placed immediately, with or without your permission.
   - Third-Party Cookies: These kinds of cookies are not placed directly by the website that you are visiting, but rather, they are placed by a third party, such as that of an

online advertiser. Because of this, these types of cookies are deemed to be more risky in nature.

3. The Purpose: The cookies in this category are as follows:

- Strictly Necessary Cookies: These kinds of cookies are actually needed in order for you to perform a certain action on a website, such as logging onto your financial institution's website. While direct consent is not required for these kinds of cookies, the GDPR highly recommends that these kinds of websites should have a detailed explanation as to why they are needed and what their specific functionalities are.

- Functionality Cookies: These types of cookies permit the website to remember the functionalities that you have performed on it in a previous session, so that the process will become more automated the next time you visit it and also do not have to do it all over again manually.

- Statistics Cookies: These are also technically referred to as "performance cookies". These kinds of cookies collect information and data that are important to the company that is hosting the website. Examples include the following:

  *How you use a website.

  *The specific pages that you have visited.

  *The links you clicked on.

  *Any other informational assets that you have may have downloaded. These include such items as whitepapers, videos, podcasts, blogs, and articles.

  It is important to note that these kinds of cookies are kept strictly anonymous. Their main objective is to provide insights to the company hosting the website on how to improve user experience and the functionality of the website.

- Marketing Cookies: These types of cookies are primarily used by marketing and advertising companies in order to see how you respond to the ads that are displayed on the website that you are currently visiting. This information is then used to deliver more focused and refined ads the next time you visit that particular website. It is important to note that this information and data can be shared with other third parties, without your explicit consent. In fact, it is this type of cookie that has received among the most contention with the GDPR.

In fact, the provisions and tenets that are found in the GDPR as it relates to cookies have their roots all the way back to 2009, under the guises of the "ePrivacy Directive", which was also passed, enacted, and enforced by the member nations of the EU. But, the important ramification here is how a business becomes compliant with the GDPR as it relates to the use of cookies. The following are the principles that must be adhered to, no matter what:

- Before any cookies can be used, the end user of the website must give explicit consent.
- Provide the needed information to the end user as to what the cookies are and how they will be used in a manner that is easy to understand and comprehend.
- Keep complete and thorough documentation of all cookies that have been used via the explicit consent of the end user.
- The end user still must be able to access the content and services provided by the website even if they do not accept the use of cookies.
- The end user has the full and complete right to withdraw their right to consent for use of the cookies at any time they wish to, without any justification or reason that needs to be provided.

The GDPR and "The Right to Be Forgotten"

As stated throughout this chapter, one of the key rights that an end user under the tenets and provisions of the GDPR is to request to have their datasets at any time they wish, but this request must be in writing and delivered to the business. In turn, the organization must abide by this and delete those datasets accordingly. This is also known technically in the GDPR as the "right to be forgotten", and it is defined as follows:

The data subject shall have the right to obtain from the controller the erasure of personal data concerning him or her without undue delay and the controller shall have the obligation to erase personal data without undue delay.

(SOURCE: https://gdpr.eu/right-to-be-forgotten/)

But what most people do not realize is that this particular "right to be forgotten" is not absolute, and even despite the request of the end user, some datasets may not even be deleted. In this section, we outline those cases in which an end-user's datasets can be deleted upon request, and those that cannot be deleted upon request.

The Cases in Which the Data Can Be Deleted upon Request

The following are the conditions in which the "right to be forgotten applies":

- The datasets are no longer needed by the business that has made use of them (in this case, the organization must then notify them of this situation).
- The right to use and process the datasets is contingent on the explicit and written consent of the end user.
- If the business claims to be using the datasets of the end user for "legitimate purposes", but there is no overriding factor, or just cause for this. If the business is still insistent on processing the datasets under this condition, it must notify the end user exactly and for what reasons the "legitimate purposes" and why then even exist in the first place.
- If the business using the datasets for marketing and advertising and the end user completely objects to this being done.
- The business has actually processed the datasets of the end user in an unlawful manner.
- If a court ruling or legal precedence explicitly states so, the datasets of the end user must be removed without question.
- If the datasets of the end-user's child or children has been used, stored, and processed, without their explicit and written consent for this to actually happen.

The Cases in Which the Data Cannot Be Deleted upon Request

These are the conditions in which the "right to be forgotten" does not apply to the following:

- The datasets are being used in the name of "freedom of expression" and the "right to free speech" by the business.
- The datasets are being processed, used, and stored in order to satisfy a specific court ruling.
- The datasets are being used to carry out an activity or action that is deemed to be in the interest of the entire public at large.
- The datasets are needed to be processed for medical emergencies and thus are needed to save the life of an individual.
- The datasets are needed to be processed for the purposes of "preventive and/or occupational medicine". Under these certain conditions, only a healthcare worker can access these datasets.
- If processing of the datasets serves these purposes:
  *They are used for scientific research in which the greater good will potentially be served.
  *They are used for historical research.
  *They are used for statistical analyses that also serve the greater good, such as conducting medical research.
  *The datasets need to be processed in Court of Law during an ongoing trial, either for the sake of the prosecution or the defense.

  Finally, the "right to be forgotten about" can be denied if the end user makes too many requests in a short time period for a business. In the end, each request by the end user in order to be "forgotten about" must be made on a case-by-case basis, as other factors, not detailed in this chapter, could also very well come into play.

If you find yourself having the need to be "forgotten about", you download the template to do so at this link:

http://cyberresources.solutions/Cyber_Compliance_Book/
RIGHT-TO-ERASURE-REQUEST-FORM.pdf

Overall, this chapter has reviewed in detail the major tenets and provisions that your business needs to be aware of when dealing with the datasets of your prospects, customers, and even employees. In the next chapter, we will provide an overview into what is deemed to be the first data privacy law that was passed in the United States. This is known as the "California Consumer Privacy Act".

Resources

1. https://www.ibm.com/topics/data-privacy
2. https://www.echr.coe.int/documents/d/echr/Convention_ENG
3. https://gdpr.eu/what-is-gdpr
4. https://gdpr.eu/data-protection-officer
5. https://www.techtarget.com/whatis/definition/privacy-policy
6. https://gdpr.eu/fines/
7. https://www.coursera.org/articles/cia-triad
8. https://usa.kaspersky.com/resource-center/definitions/cookies
9. https://gdpr.eu/right-to-be-forgotten

3

INTRODUCTION TO
THE CCPA

In Chapter 2, we reviewed the GDPR in extensive detail. As examined, it has a far-reaching implication for both businesses that are based in the European Union (EU) and those that are located overseas but still transact business there and have customers. The GDPR is deemed to be the first comprehensive data privacy legislation that has been implemented on a global basis.

One of the key advantages of the GDPR is that its sets forth a standard set of best practices and principles that all nations can follow, in an effort to reduce confusion and doubt of what exactly needs to be complied with. For example, if a business operates in both the United Kingdom and in France, there is no question of what needs to be followed in order to come into compliance with the GDPR.

But as the GDPR as evolved over time, and even especially now, this piece of legislation has actually served as a model, or even a protégé for other nations around the world to establish their own data privacy laws, that is relevant to their society and needs of the people. One of the first countries that has taken the lead in this is the United States. Each state is now coming out with its own version of the GDPR, and California is deemed to be the first state to have actually done this.

But the main problem here is that given that the United States is such a diverse country, having each state come up with their own data privacy laws can cause a great deal of confusion and even large amounts of both financial expensive and overhead in order to decide which data privacy laws need to be followed in order to come into compliance. But, this is a topic we will address at the end of this chapter, and we will now examine the rest of it in more detail what the CCPA is all about.

DOI: 10.1201/9781003496915-3

To view the entire text and legislation on the CCPA, view the following link:

http://cyberresources.solutions/Cyber_Compliance_Book/
    CCPA.pdf

The History of the CCPA

The CCPA is actually an acronym that stands for the "California Consumer Privacy Act". As its name implies, this data privacy law was enacted and passed in order to protect the datasets of consumers that physically reside in the state of California and those businesses that transact business there and have customers. It is important to note that the CCPA is also rather far-reaching, as it impacts all businesses that have a presence in the state of California. But unlike the GDPR, it does not have international jurisdiction, unless, for example, there is a business that is based in the EU that transacts business in the state of California.

The originations of the CCPA first came into existence when a data privacy group, known as the "Californians for Consumer Privacy", came together and introduced a bill that would protect the datasets of all California consumers. In full response to this, the California Department of Justice (also known as the California DOJ) approved the actual text of this bill on December 18, 2017. This then paved the way for this data privacy group to start collecting the required number of signatures that were needed so that it could be presented to the California Legislature for a robust debate on the merits of the bill.

By late 2018, there were finally enough signatures that were obtained so that the bill could be potentially passed by the California voters in the election of November 2018. It is important to note here that if a ballot were to be passed by the voters, then the California Legislature cannot amend it or revise the bill, which is technically known as the "ballot proposition". In order to avoid this kind of situation, the members of the California Legislature asked the members of the Californians for Consumer Privacy Group if they could avoid the ballot vote all together. The primary reason for this request was that if this bill were to be passed directly by the California Legislature, amendments and changes could be subsequently made to the CCPA so that it could keep with the advances not only being made in the technology that stored and processed the datasets but also so that it could keep up as well with changing dynamics of the cyber threat landscape.

Eventually, these compromises were eventually made, and the bill was passed by the California Legislature, which then became into actual law when Governor Jerry Brown signed it on June 28, 2018. It was not officially enforced until January 1, 2020.

The Intent of the CCPA

As mentioned earlier, the primary objective of the CCPA is to protect the datasets of California-based consumers. But, it is first important to define how the CCPA views what a dataset is. In the context of the actual legislation, it is technically defined as follows:

> CCPA defines personal information as information that identifies, relates to, describes, is reasonably capable of being associated with, or could reasonably be linked (directly or indirectly) with a particular consumer or household such as a real name, alias, postal address, unique personal identifier, online identifier, Internet Protocol address, email address, account name, social security number, driver's license number, license plate number, passport number, or other similar identifiers.
>
> *(SOURCE: https://en.wikipedia.org/wiki/*
> *California_Consumer_Privacy_Act)*

But, any information or data that is available in the public domain is actually considered not be as "private" or "personal"; thus, in this regard, there is no protection that is afforded by the CCPA. Even more startling is that the CCPA does not provide protection to the California consumer for these kinds of datasets:

- Personal Health Information (which are primarily used by healthcare professionals)
- Any type or kind of financial information or data (these primarily include the credit card numbers and banking information of a California resident)

The primary reason why these were not included into the CCPA was that the members of the California Legislature felt that the personal health information should be protected by HIPAA (also known as the "Health Insurance Portability And Accountability Act of 1996") and the financial information and data should be protected by the "California Financial Information Privacy", also known as the Graham-Leach-Billey Act.

When the CCPA was passed in 2018, it had three main intentions to it, which are as follows:

1. The Right to Know: Consumers that are located in the state of California have the right to have knowledge about the datasets that are being collected on them, and more importantly, how it is being processed, used, and even shared with other third-party suppliers. Examples of this include the following:
   • Under what specific categories the datasets have been collected.
   • Exactly what datasets have been collected.
   • The sources from which the datasets have been collected.
   • What is the purpose for collecting the datasets and how they will be processed.
   • The names of the third-party suppliers that the datasets will be given to.
   • If the datasets will actually be sold to other outside entities.
   All of these information must be made available upon request on an annual basis, at the minimum.
2. The Right to Delete: Consumers that are located in the state of California have the right to request a particular business that their datasets should be deleted. However, like the GDPR, this is not a guaranteed right that can be directly exercised, and it depends on the situation and the context in which the particular request is being made.
3. The Opt Out: Consumers that are located in the state of California can also request to a particular business to immediately cease sharing or selling of their datasets to other third-party suppliers, rather than simply having them deleted outright. It is important to note that this "opt out" option is only available if the datasets are being used solely for marketing and advertising

purposes. The requests for the "opt out" option remains in force for a period of one year, and only after this timeframe can a business ask a California resident to "opt-in" again.

4. The Nondiscrimination: Under its current provisions and tenets, the CCPA absolutely forbids any type or kind of discrimination against any resident of California who wishes to exercise their rights. If for any reason the consumer feels that they have been discriminated, they have the right to file a complaint directly with the Office of the California Attorney General. In this context, nondiscrimination also means that a business cannot deny a California resident the following if they exercise their rights afforded to them under the CCPA:

   • The denial to purchase goods and services.
   • Charge a different price than what was originally advertised.
   • Provide an inferior quality of the goods and services that have been purchased.

Another caveat here is that if the consumer located in California asks to have their datasets be deleted or "opted-out", and those particular datasets are absolutely necessary in the selling and procurement of goods and services, the business may not be able to offer them in the end.

Finally, the business can offer to the consumer located in California special deals, promotions, and other sorts of incentives in exchange for their datasets. But the financial value that is offered must be at least equal to or greater than the financial value of the datasets that are being requested. But if you exercise the right to "opt out" or have your datasets deleted, these incentives cannot be offered to the consumer located in California.

Amendments That Have Been Made to the CCPA

As mentioned earlier in this chapter, the original bill of the CCPA was drafted and passed by the California Legislature in a manner that allowed for future amendments. To this effect, another bill, known as the "California Privacy Rights Act of 2020", or the CPRA in short, was introduced. It is also technically known as "Proposition 24" in the California Legislature. It became the formal Legislation on January 1, 2023. Specifically, it adds two more amendments to the CCPA, which are as follows:

1. The Right to Correct: The consumer in California has the right to ask the business to change, modify, revise, or edit any of their datasets that they believe are in error or are misleading.
2. The Right to Limit: In addition to the right to "opt out", and have their datasets deleted, the consumer located in California also now as the right to request that their datasets have it use limited. An example of this would be using your Social Security Number to procure state-related services that you formally made a request to receive.
3. The Privacy Notices: Under these new amendments, entities that conduct business transactions in the state of California must also provide the relevant privacy notices to consumers whenever they submit their datasets. It is no longer optional, but is now a formal requirement that must be abided by.
4. The Data Brokers: Under the tenets and provisions of both the CCPA and the CPRA, a data broker is recognized as follows:

> A data broker (also known as an information product company) is an organization that makes money by collecting your personal information, analyzing it, and licensing it out to be used by other companies for things like marketing purposes.
>
> *(SOURCE: https://www.mcafee.com/blogs/tips-tricks/*
> *what-is-a-data-broker/)*

If any datasets are made available to these kinds of entities, they must also, without question, provide privacy notices to consumers located in California.

Finally, it is important to note that the full intent of the CPRA is not designed to replace any tenets or provisions to the CCPA, rather they are in place to further enhance them and give California residents more rights when it comes to protecting their data privacy.

The Key Differences between the GDPR and the CCPA

Many individuals and businesses assume that the GDPR and the CCPA are one and the same thing. While this is true to a certain extent in terms that they both are data privacy legislations that are designed to safeguard the datasets that have been submitted to an organization, there are key differences in them as well. In this section, we examine some the major ones, which will have the most impact to CISO and their IT security team. They are as follows:

1. Their Impact: First and foremost, the GDPR is totally comprehensive, in that it protects all sorts of datasets that are submitted, whether it is online or are physically submitted. In this regard, the GDPR is most concerned with what is known as those datasets that have been supplied by "visitor management". The technical definition of this is as follows:

   > as the act of tracking the people who come and go from your premises. As such, there is personal data collected.

   > *(SOURCE: https://www.proxyclick.com/gdpr-visitor-management)*

   But as reviewed in this chapter, the CCPA only has a direct bearing upon consumers that legally reside in California and those business that have a physical presence there as well. The only exception to this is the business that has their physical address in a different state but does financial transactions in California also. Also, the thresholds for those businesses that need to come into compliance with the CCPA are far different than that of the GDPR. These thresholds are as follows:

   • Has gross revenue of at least or greater than $25 million on an annual basis.
   • Collects, buys, processes, stores, or even sells datasets of at least 50,000 consumers that reside in California.
   • At least 50% of the gross revenue comes from selling of the datasets.
   • The datasets that are collected are from residents who reside in California.
   • The business also operates in California.

   It is important to note that the business must meet at least one of the first three criteria, whereas they must meet both of the last ones in order to be deemed as "must be compliant with the CCPA".

2. <u>What Is Protected</u>: While the protections afforded to datasets by the GDPR are very broad and all-encompassing in nature, there are two exceptions, which are as follows:
   - Any datasets that have been processed directly by the consumer themselves will not be eligible for protection.
   - If any of the above have been done primarily for personal gains or objectives, they will also not be eligible for protection.

   The GDPR also requires that written consent be provided and gives individuals the option to "opt-in" or "opt out". In contrast, the CCPA does not require written consent but must provide consumers in California with the "–opt-in" and "opt out" options.

   Also the CCPA does not afford any kind of protection to these datasets if they belong to any of these categories:
   - The datasets are already publicly available.
   - Any datasets that are protected under the following pieces of legislation:
     *The Confidentiality of Medical Information Act (also known as the CMIA)
     *The Federal Health Insurance Portability and Accountability Act (also known as the HIPAA)

3. <u>The Processing</u>: It is important to note that under both the CCPA and the GDPR, personal datasets can be technically defined as follows:

   Any information that can directly or indirectly represent an identifiable person.

   (SOURCE: https://www.proxyclick.com/blog/ gdpr-and-ccpa-compliance-5-differences)

   But when it comes to the actual processing of datasets, the two pieces of legislation are actually quite different. For example, with the GDPR, the processing of datasets includes the following acts:
   - The collection of the actual datasets
   - Reorganizing the datasets into a coherent and logical format

- Making the datasets available, in a very secure manner, to all of the required stakeholders that are actually involved in the processing of the datasets
- The subsequent removal and permanent deletion of datasets from the databases, whether they are physical or virtual, or even a combination of both

Under the CCPA, the processing of datasets are as follows:

- The collection of datasets can take place through any means, as long as it has been secured so that it cannot be intercepted by a malicious third party.
- Processing is only defined when there is some sort of manipulation to the datasets that have actually occurred.
- The selling of the datasets does not have to be defined as an actual financial transaction. Rather, it can also involve the "trading" of the datasets directly to a third-party supplier, but only if the consumer residing in California has been notified ahead of this intended action, and its only being done to serve their best interests.

4. <u>What Must Be Provided</u>: Under the tenets and the provisions of both the GDPR and the CCPA, consumers residing in both California and the EU nations must be provided with the following pieces of information:

- How the datasets are being shared with third-party suppliers and why this is happening.
- The nature and purpose of why their datasets are being processed, and how they will benefit from this kind of activity.
- The exact rights that consumers in both California and the nations in the EU have regarding their datasets, and how those rights can be exercised. Also, a point of contact must be specified for consumers to reach out to directly.

But in terms of the differences, these are as follows, with the CCPA:

- The consumers who reside in California must be notified of all of the above, even after a year has passed. This includes how and why their datasets were sold to a third-party supplier.

- They must also be notified in writing if a third-party supplier is either selling or transferring their datasets to another or different third-party supplier.

Here are the differences with the GDPR:

- The consumer must be notified in real time about any activity happening with their datasets. This includes storage, archiving, selling, processing, or transfer to a third-party supplier.
- How long their datasets can be held and retained by a particular business, and more importantly, if any automated tools, such as generative AI, machine learning, or neural networks, will be used to process them.
- They also must be informed on a regular basis of their right to have their datasets deleted or to "opt out" at any time. Furthermore, the consumer is absolutely under no obligation to provide the business holding their datasets with reasons for these actions.
- If a third-party supplier is going to process the datasets of the consumer, they must be notified directly in writing within a 30-day timespan, and the exact means as to how the third-party supplier actually got a hold of their datasets. For example, was it sold or transferred to them from the point of origination?

5. The Financial Penalties: In this particular category, both the CCPA and the GDPR have steep financial penalties for those businesses that do not come into compliance with these pieces of legislation or simply do not abide the provisions and tenets of them. Chapter 2 on GDPR reviewed in extensive detail the financial penalties with that, but in terms of the CCPA, they are as follows:

- $2,500.00 per violation for every dataset record that was in violation of the CCPA.
- $7,500.00 per violation for every dataset record that was in violation of the CCPA *__that was intentional__*.
- A minimum of $750.00 and greater for violations of the CCPA that are brought as a civil lawsuit into a Court of Law.

- The affected resident in California also has the right to file a lawsuit; however, they are primarily responsible for hiring their own attorney to prosecute the lawsuit.

So as you can see, the bottom line is that the GDPR is much more proactive than the CCPA when it comes to safeguarding the datasets and the rights that consumers have in this regard.

For a more detailed comparison between the GDPR and the CCPA, visit the following link:

http://cyberresources.solutions/Cyber_Compliance_Book/
  GDPR_CCPA_Comparison-Guide.pdf

The Differences in the Datasets

As noted earlier, the GDPR has a rather broad definition of what a dataset really is. But, under the tenets and provisions of the CCPA, two distinctions are made in this regard, which are important to be aware of. They are as follows:

- The Personal Information: These are datasets that can be tied either directly to an individual and/or their family. Examples of these include the following:
  *Full legal name
  *The social security number(s)
  *The Email address(es)
  *Online transactions of products and services that have been purchased
  *Web browsing history
  *The geolocation data
  *Biometrics, such as fingerprints, etc.
  *Social media profiles
- The Sensitive Personal Information: These are the pieces of meta data that are considered to be a subset of the actual datasets. Examples of these include the following:
  *Social security numbers
  *Financial account information
  *Debit card/credit card information
  *Passwords and other forms of login credentials.

*Contents related to postal mail, Email, and text messages.
*Healthcare information and data
*Sexual orientation
*Racial/ethnicity information and data
*Religious affiliations

If a Violation of the CCPA Has Occurred

Although it was discussed earlier that the consumer in California does have a right to file a lawsuit, it is not always the most favorable option to choose from the outset. The primary reason for this is that there are certain conditions in which one take this action. The main one is if the PII (personal identifiable information) datasets have been directly stolen or hijacked from the consumer. Examples of these kinds of datasets include the following:

- The social security number
- Any federal or state government issued ID, which include:
  *The Driver's License Number
  *The Tax Identification Number.
  *The Passport Number.
  *The Military Identification Number.
  *Any other type or kind of unique identification number that has been issued on a government-related document, which is also used to identify the consumer in California.
  *Any kind of financial data which includes:
    →Credit card numbers
    →Banking account numbers
    →Debit card numbers
- Any sort of medically related PII datasets
- Any kind of biometric template that has been submitted, stored, and processed by a biometric modality. Examples of these include the following:
  *The fingerprint
  *Images of the iris and/or the retina
  *Images of the face
  *Recordings of the voice, signature, or keystroke patterns
  *Images of the hand

Also, the following conditions must be met before you can file a lawsuit against the business:

- The PII datasets must have been intercepted, stolen, or hijacked in a format that was unencrypted and "nonredacted".
- The PII datasets must have been intercepted, stolen, or hijacked as a result of a security breach in which the business did not deploy or upgrade the controls that were needed.
- The consumer in California must provide written notification to the business of the exact section of the CCPA which has been violated, and they must give that entity no later than thirty days to respond to it.
- If the business has responded to say that the appropriate mitigation steps have been taken and that the appropriate controls have been deployed and put into place, then the lawsuit cannot take forth. This must be sent to the consumer in California in a written format.
- Despite the above, if the same violation still happens, then the consumer in California can file a lawsuit, no matter what the circumstances are.

For all other violations, the only recourse for the consumer in California to take is to file a complaint directly with the attorney general of California. But, it is important to keep in mind that they will not necessarily act on just a single complaint, but if there are many of them that are of similar nature, only then will it take any sort of legal action. When filing a complaint, the consumer in California must be very specific in the violation that has occurred, the time it happened, and how it actually occurred.

In Chapter 4, we cover another data privacy law, but it serves a different purpose and application. It is called the CMMC, and it has been established by the Department of Defense, also known as the DoD. It requires that defense contractors and their subcontractors have to make sure that they have the needed controls deployed into place to safeguard what are known as "controlled unclassified information" and "federal contract information".

Resources

1. https://en.wikipedia.org/wiki/California_Consumer_Privacy_Act
2. https://www.mcafee.com/blogs/tips-tricks/what-is-a-data-broker/
3. https://www.proxyclick.com/gdpr-visitor-management
4. https://www.proxyclick.com/blog/gdpr-and-ccpa-compliance-5-differences

4

AN OVERVIEW OF
THE CMMC

Chapters 2 and 3 of this book have extensively reviewed two key data privacy laws, namely the GDPR and the CCPA. Although these are the major ones, it should be noted that other forms of data privacy laws abound not just in the United States, but also in other countries. The primary reason for this is that the world is becoming very much interconnected, driven by the digital nature of the devices that we use today. Because of this, consumers on a global basis are becoming more cognizant of how their datasets are being used and are demanding rights over how they can be used and controlled.

But it is not just the business community around the world that is need of data privacy laws; even the federal government here in the United States is in need of them. This is clearly evident with the Department of Defense (also known as the "DoD"). Among all the branches and agencies of the federal government, the DoD is likely the largest issuer of bids and contracts to the private industry.

Because of this, a lot of confidential and private information is being shared by the federal government with the private sector. This includes what is technically known as "controlled unclassified information" (also known as "CUI") and "federal classified information" (also known as FCI). To make sure that necessary controls are in place to protect these two key pieces of datasets, the DoD has mandated the implementation of what is known as the "CMMC".

In simpler terms, the private sector must achieve a certain level of certification mandated by the DoD before they are even allowed to place bids or even be awarded federal government contracts. This is the focal point of this chapter.

The CMMC

As described, the CMMC is a data privacy law that has been set forth and mandated by the DoD. It is an actually an acronym that stands for the "Cybersecurity Maturity Model Certification". Although the CMMC is quite complex in nature, it serves one main purpose—to make sure that the required controls are in place by the private sector to protect both the FCI and CUI datasets that are entrusted to the businesses by the DoD.

These types of datasets are provided by the DoD so that the private sector can make use of them in order to create and deliver the products and services that are specified in the federal government contracts awarded. At present time, there are two versions of the CMMC and they both have been appropriately labeled as "CMMC 1.0" and "CMMC 2.0", respectively, which will be reviewed in this chapter. But first, it is important to give an overview of what the private sector really is for the CMMC.

The Defense Industrial Base

The main private sector that serves the needs of the DoD and other related federal government agencies is what is known as the "Defense Industrial Base", also known as DIB in short. As the name implies, these are primarily the defense contractors that reside not just here in the United States but also on a global basis. Examples of these entities include the following:

- The Lockheed Martin Corporation
- The Raytheon Technologies Corporation
- The General Dynamics Corporation
- The Pfizer Inc.
- The Boeing Company
- The Northrop Grumman Corporation
- The Humana Inc.
- The Hill Corporation
- The L3 Harris Technologies Inc.
- The BAE Systems PLC

Although at the present time these are the ten largest defense contractors, there others as well, and they too must come into compliance with the CMMC. Unlike the GDPR and the CCPA, where there are certain thresholds (such as employee size and revenue size) that determine if a business has to compliance with the tenets and provisions of them, any entity that wishes to do business with the DoD must also come into compliance with the CMMC. There are no other absolute thresholds for this criteria. This even includes the subcontractors that also provide support to the main defense contractors. Examples of these include the following:

- Entities in research and engineering
- Entities that are involved in the development of new system designs
- Entities that are involved in the acquirement and procurement of the raw materials needed
- Entities that are involved in the final production and delivery of newer products and services

In the end, there are well over 300,000 entities just in the DIB by itself. Before diving further into the mechanics of the CMMC 1.0, is important to provide more background into both the FCI and CUI datasets, which are what the next two sections are about.

The CUI Datasets

Simply put, CUI are those datasets that have value to them, and, in the strictest, are confidential and private in nature. This is where the "classified" part of the acronym comes into play. But, they can also be made available to those people who are authorized to have them. This is where the "unclassified" comes into effect. But this comes only under the jurisdiction of "lawful government purposes". This is technically defined as follows:

> Any activity, mission, function, operation, or endeavor that the U.S. Government authorizes or recognizes as within the scope of its legal authorities or the legal authorities of a nonexecutive branch entity.
>
> *(SOURCE: https://www.dodcui.mil/Portals/109/Documents/Info %20Paper%20on%20DoD%20CUI%20Program.pdf?ver= De5b7M5cuVTQtuo11DId5A%3D%3D).*

So with this definition in mind, the following individuals can be authorized to have direct access to the CUI datasets:

- Direct members of Congress
- State and local government entities that have an affiliation with the DoD or the federal government in some way, shape, or form
- Tribal units that belong to the federal government
- Companies that are classified to be in the DIB and have been awarded a DoD contract
- Certain people in the academia who are involved with conducting high-level research for the DoD or the federal government

How the CUI Datasets Can Be Handled

Given the sort of liberal nature of CUI datasets, there is also more latitude as to how they can be handled. The following are these types of scenarios:

- The CUI datasets can be shared with no limitations in the Congressional Meetings.
- The CUI datasets can be distributed while the Congress is in real-time session.
- Any materials marked as "CUI" can be kept and retained by any member of the executive branch of the federal government for a "reasonable" time period.
- Any member of Congress who has attended and participated in an actual Congressional Meeting can also request to have access and retention of the CUI datasets for a "reasonable" time period.

The Types of CUI Labels

In the world of CUI, there are two types of labels that can be applied, which are as follows:

1. <u>Legislative Materials</u>: These are commonly referred to as "LMI". They are designed to protect information or data related to pieces of legislation that are still under review by members of Congress. It can also be used to protect

inquiries that are placed upon the DoD and the responses provided to them.

2. <u>Committee Use Only</u>: CUI materials that have this kind of label attached to them means that only the members of a certain Congressional Committee should access and view these documents. But if other members of Congress need to access these kinds of materials, the committee can place a special request with the DoD to have this label removed.

The FCI Datasets

The next grouping of datasets that the DoD entrust, or intends to once compliance has been achieved with a defense contractor, are known as "FCI". The technical definition for them is as follows:

> FCI is "Information not intended for public release. It is provided by or generated by for the Government under a contract to develop or deliver a product or service to the Government. FCI does not include information provided by the Government to the public.

(SOURCE: https://www.cmmcaudit.org/what-is-fci-in-cmmc/)

In other words, although the CUI datasets can be shared freely with other members of the federal government with restrictions, FCI datasets cannot be shared with anyone unless they have been fully vetted and authorized by the DoD to access and view such datasets. So, if the DoD were to entrust a defense contractor with FCI datasets, they must first reach a certain level of trust by obtaining a degree of certification with the CMMC.

Also, the FCI datasets have a much narrower scope than the CUI datasets (as reviewed in the last section). They are strictly produced, shared, and processed so that a tangible good or service can be delivered to the DoD per the exact terms of the contract that was awarded through the bidding process. By their nature, FCI datasets are not strictly quantitative; they can also be qualitative. Examples of these include the following:

- Any Emails transmitted between the DoD and the defense contractor (and vice versa)

- Any other policies that are needed by the defense contractor in order to fulfill the terms of the contract that was awarded by the DoD
- Any other pieces of tangible content, such as those found in instant messaging, video conferencing, SMS messages, and so on

The Levels at Which the FCI Is Implemented

As reviewed in this chapter, from within the CMMC 1.0, there are five levels of maturity; but in the CMMC 2.0, there are only two. But, with specific regard to the FCI datasets, it impacts only the first two levels which are as follows:

1. Level One: This is deemed to be the initial phase where there is no formal structure yet in place in order to accomplish the goals of the contact that were awarded by the DoD. Instead, the approach is ad hoc until it is all formalized. These typically can include the first round of meetings, information/data gathering, preliminary analysis requirements, question and answer sessions, and so on.
2. Level Two: At this level, the workflows and processes that are needed to fulfill the terms of the DoD contract become much more solidified and defined. In other words, the ability to track in more detail what is happening can now take place. This also involves the following activities:
   - The implementation of various costing schedules that are related to the work tasks
   - The scheduling of workflows between the defense contractor and their respective subcontractors
   - Defining the functionalities of the established workflows (in other words, defining in further detail the output that is expected, with an emphasis on the FCI-related datasets that are to be created when developing the goods or services for the federal government)

The CMMC 1.0

This framework for the first version of the CMMC was launched by the Office of the Under Secretary of Defense for Acquisition and

Sustainment, specifically known as the OUSD(AS) in short. Another significant theoretical component of the CMMC 1.0 is the "NIST SP 800-171". From within these initial federal government initiatives and documents, the CMMC 1.0 was created by implementing seventeen security domains, which are as follows:

1. Access Control (AC): This defines the rights, privileges, and permissions that will be assigned to each and every employee of the defense contractor and their associated subcontractors in order to fulfill the terms of the DoD contract. This will also define who can access the CUI and FCI datasets both remotely and internally. Following the concept of "least privilege" is highly encouraged for this particular domain.

2. Asset Management (AM): You must have the ability and processes to document both your physical and digital assets that are used to fulfill the terms of the DoD contract.

3. Audit and Accountability (AU): This specifies the processes that you have in place for recording and logging all of the network activities of the employees of both the defense contractor and their subcontractors. Further, you also need to establish a specific process as to how an audit will be carried out and who will be doing that particular audit.

4. Awareness and Training (AT): This specifies that a security awareness training program (as many as needed) must be given on a regular basis to the employees of both the defense contractor and their subcontractors. Special emphasis must be placed on how to securely store and process both the CUI and FCI datasets that have been transferred over by the DoD.

5. Configuration Management (CM): This specifies that a system must be put in place to formally approve and record any changes that have taken place to both the physical and digital assets used to house and process both the CUI and FCI datasets.

6. Identification and Authentication (IA): This specifies that the proper roles and titles must be assigned to employees of both the defense contractor and the subcontractor for accessing and processing the FCI and CUI datasets that have been handed over by the DoD. Furthermore, it is expected that the concept of "Role-Based Access Control", also known as "RBAC", will be fully observed. This simply means that each job title will

have relevant rights, permissions, and privileges assigned to them, and no more than that.

7. Incident Response (IR): Both the defense contractor and their associated subcontractors must have an incident response plan in place to contain and further mitigate any security breaches resulting in the data exfiltration of both the FCI and CUI datasets, whether they were the primary target of the cyberattacker or not.

8. Maintenance (MA): This specifies that a plan must be put in place that details how you will maintain the upkeep of both your physical and digital assets that reside from within your IT and network infrastructure. With regard to this, there must be a special emphasis on how software patches and upgrades will be installed and deployed, and the schedule that will be adhered to.

9. Media Protection (MP): This relates primarily to portable storage devices used to store both FCI and CUI datasets, such as USB drives or other mediums used to store these datasets into cloud-based deployments such as Microsoft Azure, or AWS. Furthermore, you must have a media protection plan in place which addresses the following:
   - How the media devices will be protected
   - How they will be "sanitized" when they are no longer needed
   - Any protocols in place to ensure the protection of media devices when they are physically or virtually transported from one destination to another point of destination.

10. Personnel Security (PS): This specifies that you have the necessary protocols in place in order to make sure that employees and contractors are fully vetted before they are hired, and that they have been fully and completely trained in how to properly and securely store and process both the FCI and CUI datasets they are entrusted with. Also, you must demonstrate that after an employee or contractor leaves for whatever reason, their access to the datasets is fully and immediately terminated.

11. Physical Protection (PE): This specifies how the actual physical infrastructure of the defense contractor and their associated subcontractors are secured, both externally and internally.

Further, you have to show evidence that you have the necessary protocols in place to confirm the identity of the employees before they are permitted to enter inside the physical infrastructure.

12. Recovery (RE): This specifies the details of your backup plan and how they will be used to restore both the FCI and CUI datasets to their full level of integrity after a security breach. This plan also needs to specify the schedule that your IT security team will follow when making the backups and how and where they will be stored, either on premises or in a cloud-based deployment, or even a hybrid-based approach.

13. Risk Management (RM): This specifies the exact risk assessment methodology that you will make use of in order to identify the vulnerabilities and gaps that are found in both your physical and digital assets. Further, you also need the tools as to how this will be done (such as vulnerability scanning and/or penetration testing) and how these gaps and weaknesses will be remediated. Finally, you also need to specify the ranking system that you will use to categorize the exact level of vulnerability that each physical and digital asset are exposed to.

14. Security Assessment (CA): This specifies as to how you and your IT security team will carry out the daily cybersecurity activities in order to ensure that your lines of defenses are as "beefed up" as possible, on a real-time basis. Also, you will need to have a plan as to how the controls will be deployed and upgraded, when and as needed.

15. Situational Awareness (SA): This specifies the details of the threat-monitoring system that you currently have in place and how it will be upgraded and kept current. Typical examples of this is the assessment of log files that have been outputted by your network security devices, and having them further analyzed by an artificial intelligence tool and presented in a coherent manner via an SIEM (also known as a "Security Incident and Event Manager") software package.

16. System and Communication Protection (SC): This specifies how both your physical and digital assets are protected when they "communicate" with each other, as well as how your network lines of communications are made secure between

the place of business of the defense contractor and their subcontractors, their remote workforce, and even internal communicators.

17. System and Information Integrity (SI): This specifies how you and your IT security team will manage and correct any technical flaws that may suddenly occur in both your physical and digital assets. This also includes the close monitoring of any necessary "bouncing back" of rogue content and data packets that try to make their way into your IT and network infrastructure.

The Maturity Levels of the CMMC 1.0

It is very important to note that each of the seventeen domains, as described in the last section, are governed by what are known as "maturity levels". In the CMMC 1.0, there were five of them, which are as follows:

1. Maturity Level 1 ("Basic Cyber Hygiene"): This specifies the needed levels of "cyber hygiene" in order for a defense contractor and their subcontractors to be entrusted with the handling of the FCI datasets only.

2. Maturity Level 2 ("Intermediate Cyber Hygiene"): This specifies that the defense contractor and their associated subcontractors have exhibited more sophisticated levels of "cyber hygiene" and therefore can be entrusted with more and varied FCI datasets.

3. Maturity Level 3 ("Good Cyber Hygiene"): This specifies that the defense contractor and their associated subcontractors have exhibited a complete and total display of all the needed required levels of cyber hygiene. This means that that they can be entrusted with all kinds and types of FCI datasets.

4. Maturity Level 4 ("Proactive Cyber Hygiene"): This specifies that the defense contractor and their associated subcontractors have practiced enough "cyber hygiene" that they can now be entrusted with access to the CUI datasets.

5. Maturity Level 5 ("Proactive Cyber Hygiene"): This specifies that the defense contractor and their associated subcontractors

have exhibited even advanced levels of "cyber hygiene" and, as a result, they can be entrusted with access to all kinds and types of CUI datasets. It also demonstrates that they can protect both the FCI and CUI datasets from what are known as "advanced persistent threats", also known as an APT in short. This can be technically defined as follows:

> An advanced persistent threat (APT) is a sophisticated, sustained cyberattack in which an intruder establishes an undetected presence in a network in order to steal sensitive data over a prolonged period of time.
>
> *(SOURCE: https://www.crowdstrike.com/cybersecurity-101/ advanced-persistent-threat-apt/).*

At this stage, a defense contractor and their subcontractors must be certified at any point in these maturity levels. However, the level of certification required depends on the goals and objectives of the defense contractor and subcontractors when bidding on DoD contracts. It should also be noted that a defense contractor and their associated subcontractors cannot start at any maturity level they desire.

Rather, they have to start by getting certified at maturity level 1 and work their way up to higher maturity levels in an incremental fashion, as each level builds upon the previous one. Most defense contractors and their subcontractors aspire to be certified at least at maturity level 3.

These five Maturity Levels are reviewed in the matrix below:

Maturity Level	Model	Assessor
Maturity Level 1	17 Practice Areas	3rd Party
Maturity Level 2	72 Practice Areas	Not Needed
Maturity Level 3	130 Practice Areas	3rd Party
Maturity Level 4	156 Practice Areas	Not Needed
Maturity Level 5	171 Practice Areas	3rd Party

Figure 4.1

Notes to the above matrix:

- A practice area consists of specific activities that need to be accomplished in order to receive certification at a particular maturity level. Ultimately, these activities support the domains of CMMC 1.0 as just reviewed. In total, there are 171 practice areas within CMMC 1.0.

- Under CMMC 1.0, although the defense contractor and their associated subcontractors could self-assess if they have met all of the requirements for certification at a particular maturity level, it had to be verified by an independent third party, hence the column entitled "Assessor". This could be done either with a "Certified CMMC Assessor" (also known as a CCA) or a "Certified Third-Party Assessor" (also known as a C3PAO). The latter is actually accredited by what is known as the "CMMC Accreditation Body" (also known as the CMMC-AB).

The CMMC 2.0

The Constraints

When CMMC 1.0 first came out and the defense contractors and their associated subcontractors started the certification process, many complaints were relayed to the DoD. Some of the main complaints included the following:

1. The Time Involved: For many of these entities, trying to come into compliance with the CMMC and get the respective certification took too much time. Although at this time, the defense contractor and their associated subcontractors only had to reach maturity level 3 in order to gain complete access to the FCI datasets, there were many steps involved in the process. This led many to question whether the time and effort were worth it.

2. The Self-Assessments: Although the defense contractors and their associated subcontractors could self-attest that all of the needed controls were in place to safeguard both the CUI and FCI datasets, this still had to be validated by a third-party assessor. If any discrepancies were found, this meant that the entities had to go and start all over again with double-checking all of their controls that were already in place and deployed.

3. Full Agreement: Before a certification by the DoD could be issued to the defense contractor and their associated subcontractors, all individuals involved in the entire process had to

come into agreement with the results of the self-assessment and the validation of the third-party assessor. If any untruths were represented, this became technically known as a "false claim", and, thus, would trigger a huge and exhaustive audit by the DoD. Also, any type or kind of "false claims" would also come under the Department of Justice (also known as the "DoJ"), under the guises of the Civil Cyber-Fraud Initiative. The rationale behind this is that any control that is not fully optimized constitutes a potential data privacy breach, which is addressed under this legislation.

Because of all of this and the huge expense that was borne by the defense contractor and their associated subcontractors, the DoD mandated that there should be only three formal maturity levels so that certification could be awarded, as well as the contracts, in order to keep up with the workflow and the projects that the DoD was aspiring to keep with.

The Maturity Levels of the CMMC 2.0

So now, there are only the three levels of maturity versus the five levels of maturity that were in the CMMC 2.0. These new maturity levels can now be defined as follows:

1. Maturity Level 1 ("The Foundational Level"): This formulates the groundwork for what actually defines what basic "cyber hygiene" is truly all about. Thus, only the minimal amount of controls are thus needed for the full protection and safeguarding of the FCI datasets. This is also stipulated in the document entitled "Basic Safeguarding of Covered Contractor Information Systems", also known as the "48 CFR 52.204-21". But, there must also be a specific plan in place that demonstrates how these controls will not only be deployed, but also upgraded over time, when and as needed.

2. Maturity Level 2 ("The Advanced Level"): This particular level is deemed to be the "stepping stone" for achieving a baseline and the minimal number of controls that are necessary in order to gain access to, store, and process the CUI datasets, along with the FCI datasets.

3. <u>Maturity Level 3 ("The Expert Level")</u>: This particular level mandates that the fullest and maximum amount of controls that are needed to protect and safeguard both the CUI and FCI datasets are now completely required. It is only after that certification has been achieved at this level that the defense contractors and their associated subcontractors can bid upon and be awarded those contracts that deal with the nation's most critical defense programs.

Additional Domains

Also in the CMMC 2.0, there have been three new domains included, in addition to those that were reviewed under the section of CMMC 1.0. They are as follows:

- The Penetration Resistant Architecture
- The Damage Limiting Operations
- The Cyber Resiliency Survivability

Other Changes to the CMMC 2.0

In addition to only having three distinct maturity levels, there are also some other changes that have been made. The biggest ones have been in the way that the defense contractors and their associated subcontractors now have to be certified. This is detailed as follows:

1. <u>At Maturity Level 1</u>: At this level, the defense contractors and the subcontractors can now self-attest that all the needed controls have been indeed put in place and fully optimized for the protection and safeguarding of both the FCI and CUI datasets. However, this also has to be approved by the C-Suite. As a result, there is no longer a need for a "Certified CMMC Assessor" to provide any further validation.
2. <u>At Maturity Level 2</u>: At this level, self-assessments and attestations can also be done by the defense contractors and their associated contractors, but if any CUI datasets are to be stored and processed by them, then validation is needed by a "Certified CMMC Assessor".

3. <u>At Maturity Level 3</u>: At this level, the defense contractors and their associated subcontractors need to only have their maturity level 3 certification renewed every three years, but it must be done by a "Certified Third-Party Assessor". Also, any self-assessments and attestations must be further validated by a "Certified CMMC Assessor".

The Use of Waivers and POA&Ms

Another key change to the CMMC 2.0 versus the CMMC 1.0 is the use of what are known as "waivers" and the "plans of actions and milestones" (also known as POA&M in short). These are tools to self-assessment and attestations that the defense contractors and their associated subcontractors can also make use of. But, the important caveat here is that these documents must have an actionable set of items that show how the gaps and vulnerabilities that were found in the controls will be remediated.

In fact, the POA&M was not even allowed with the CMMC 1.0. But, this particular document must have concrete and absolute deadlines. Also, the DoD highly recommends that the defense contractors and their associated subcontractors follow closely the tenets and provisions that are set forth by the NIST Special Publication 800-171. This document can be downloaded from the following link:

http://cyberresources.solutions/Cyber_Compliance_Book/ NIST_800_172.pdf

Finally, the processes that have been reviewed in this section cannot be used for the following activities, as mandated by the DoD:

- Anything related to identity and authentication management processes or processes
- Any security awareness training programs that you have launched or planned
- Any audits that are related to the protection and safeguarding of both the CUI and FCI datasets
- Any techniques related to portable storage device destruction
- Any risk assessments that have been conducted or are planned for the future

The Maturity Levels in the CMMC 2.0 are outlined in the matrix below:

Maturity Level	Model	Assessor
Maturity Level 1	17 practice areas	Self Assessment
Maturity Level 2	72 practice areas	Self-Assessment/some third-party assessments needed for critical infrastructure bids and contract awarding
Maturity Level 3	130 practice areas	Third party, done every 3 years

Figure 4.2

In Chapter 5, we will outline the steps that you and your IT security team can take to prepare for compliance with the GDPR, CCPA, and CMMC.

Resources

1. https://www.dodcui.mil/Portals/109/Documents/Info%20Paper%20on%20DoD%20CUI%20Program.pdf?ver=De5b7M5cuVTQtuo11DId5A%3D%3D
2. https://www.cmmcaudit.org/what-is-fci-in-cmmc
3. https://www.crowdstrike.com/cybersecurity-101/advanced-persistent-threat-apt

5

HOW TO COME INTO COMPLIANCE WITH THE DATA PRIVACY LAWS

So far in this book, we have covered the following topics:

- The importance of data and datasets and their particular relevance to data privacy laws
- An overview into the GDPR
- An overview into the CCPA
- An overview into the CMMC

While we have covered the major tenets and provisions for each of the abovementioned data privacy laws, the next question that often comes to mind is how does a business actually come into full compliance with them. It is important to keep in mind that it is not the GDPR, CCPA, and the CMMC that affects all businesses. For example, with regard to the first two, the two defining criteria are as follows:

- The employee size of the business
- The revenue size of the business

As reviewed throughout this book, there are certain thresholds to the aforementioned two criteria. In the end, if the business in question meets at least one of the thresholds and criteria, they are bound to the provisions and tenets of the ones which affect them. But with regard to the CMMC, the only businesses that are affected by it are those that wish to conduct transactions with the DoD. This primarily affects the defense contractors and their associated subcontractors.

It is very important for a business to come into any kind of data privacy law that affects, not just the GDPR, CCPA, and CMMC. If

DOI: 10.1201/9781003496915-5

compliance is not reached, that particular business could face a rather time-consuming and exhaustive audit, as well as face harsh financial penalties.

It should also be noted that a business should not "go at it alone" when attempting to come into compliance with these data privacy laws. Rather, they should seek the help of a cybersecurity firm that actually specializes in doing this. True, there will be some cost that is associated with this, far outweighing the costs of trying to survive an actual audit and facing even harsher financial penalties in the end.

With this in mind, the goal of this chapter is to provide some general steps and guidance as to how you should prepare for these data privacy laws. They are by no means inclusive, and the main intention of this chapter is to provide some sort of framework for you and your IT security team to follow as you establish your compliance plans. We will first start off with the CMMC.

Coming into Compliance with the CMMC

A general framework that you can use to get ideas for your compliance plan is as follows:

1. Assess Your CUI Environment: As it was reviewed in the last chapter, coming into compliance with the CMMC means that you have to reach and obtain certification at a particular maturity level. One of the best ways to do this is to document and deploy the right kinds and types of controls that you are planning to deploy in order to protect and safeguard both the CUI and FCI datasets. One of the best ways to get started with this is to assess the particular environment in which you will be storing and processing the FCI and CUI datasets. The same also needs to be done of your associated subcontractors, as they will be handling these kinds of mission critical datasets as well. Another key factor that you will need to pay very careful attention to is to how these datasets will be transmitted from the point of origin to the point of destination, and vice versa.

2. Compile the Documentation: You and your IT security team will need to prepare complete documentation that clearly details as to you and your associated subcontractors will implement

the needed controls to protect and safeguard both the CUI and FCI datasets This will include (but not limited to) the creation of best practices, standards, and how the controls will be audited and monitored. In order to optimize this entire documentation process, it is important to take a hierarchical methodology.

3. Define the Plans: When it comes to the CMMC, there are two distinct sets of documentation that must be updated on real-time basis, no matter what the circumstance be. These are as follows:

   • The SSP: This is an acronym for "systems security plan". Its primary intention is to serve as a "database" of sorts as to the defense contractor and their associated subcontractors, the processes, and technology of which they are embracing for both the CUI and FCI datasets. Any changes to any or all of them need to be documented here.

   • The POA&M: As reviewed Chapter 4, this is an acronym for "plans of actions and milestones". It is also meant to serve specifically to what is known as a "risk register". For instance, any deficiencies, gaps, or vulnerabilities that have been found in the controls need to be thoroughly documented here, as well as the actions that took place to remediate the situation(s).

4. Avoid the Data Sprawl: Most of the time, defense contractors and their associated subcontractors deal with very large FCI and CUI datasets, which is primarily dependent on the size, scope, and nature of the contract that were awarded by the DoD. For example, the datasets are typically stored and accessed across a wide myriad of storage devices, which include both databases and portable devices. By having so many disparate sources at hand, this greatly increases the attack surface for cyberattackers to penetrate into. Therefore, the solution here is to centralize all your CUI and FCI datasets into one central repository wherever possible.

5. Break It Down: There is no doubt that achieving CMMC certification can be a very daunting task. As a result, many C3PAOs recommend breaking down these larger tasks into much smaller ones, so that it will become much more

manageable to deal with. If you do not do this, you and your IT security team will feel completely overwhelmed, and as a result, mistakes will most likely be made, which, of course, you will want to avoid at all costs.

Coming into Compliance with the GDPR and CCPA

The compliance techniques described in the last section for the CMMC can also be applied to varying degrees to both the CCPA and the GDPR. But, however, keep in mind that that these two data privacy laws do not deal specifically with the CUI and FCI datasets. But, the techniques later are highly advised to be used when achieving compliance with both the GDPR and the CCPA. They are as follows:

1. The Data Mapping: This technique is often done by the team of database administrator. It can be technically defined as follows:

   Data mapping is the process of matching data fields in one database to corresponding data fields in another—helping the two databases communicate and share data more effectively.

   (SOURCE: https://transcend.io/blog/data-mapping-basics)

   In other words, correlating datasets stored in two different database environments may not seem necessary at first glance, and in fact, it is not required by the GDPR or the CCPA. But by doing this exercise will allow you, the CISO, and your IT security team the chance to fully comprehend and document the locations of all your datasets. This is one of the first questions that you will be asked if you ever face an audit by a data privacy regulator.

2. Be Certain of the Vendors: Whenever you contract out any dataset storage and processing activities with a third-party supplier, you must first thoroughly vet them out first. This is also expected to take place, according to the tenets of the GDPR and the CCPA. But remember one thing here: If the third-party supplier experiences a security breach and if any of the datasets that you have entrusted them to become impacted, they will not be held responsible and accountable

for it, but you will be. So that is why you have to take every possible precaution ahead of time in order to ensure that the IT and network infrastructure is at least as secure as yours.

3. <u>Always Have a Privacy Policy</u>: Although privacy policies are not yet fully mandated by the GDPR or the CCPA, it is always best to have them available to your end users on a 24 × 7 × 365 basis. Most importantly, make sure that your privacy policies are always updated with the latest information and how it could possibly impact your end users.

4. <u>Be Responsive</u>: Even if your business does not fall under the tenets and provisions of the GDPR and the CCPA, given the way the world is today, you will most likely be asked by your end users about their datasets. It is very important that you respond to them quickly, and in writing. If the response is not timely, you could find your business under the radar of data privacy regulators.

5. <u>Avoid Data Sprawl</u>: This was also reviewed in the last section, with regard to the CMMC. Simply put, it will be best practice if you only collect those datasets from your end users as needed and discard them as quickly as possible once you are done using them. Not only will this decrease the attack surface of the cyberattacker, but the chances of a data exfiltration attack happening to your business will be greatly reduced.

6. <u>Security Awareness Training</u>: For those employees that will be intimately involved with the day-to-day storage and processing of the datasets, it is imperative that you give them the needed training on a regular basis and always be reminding them of the consequences if they do not maintain good levels of "cyber hygiene". Also, in order to make sure that your employees are truly applying what they have learned, you can also launch mock security breaches to see how they will respond truly. A good example of this is a mock phishing attack. By doing this, you can see how many employees have actually fallen for it, thus giving you a clear indication of how your security awareness training programs need to be improved, or those specific employees that need more of it.

7. <u>Keeping All Informed</u>: Even if you have not been a victim of a security breach, it is always a good idea to inform your

end users of what exactly is going on with their datasets. It is important that this be sent out in writing, whether it is by the traditional mail or even Email. By doing this practice, if you are ever faced with an audit by a data privacy regulator, you will have the documentation readily available to prove that you have done your "due diligence".

8. Keep Track of the Logs: The log files that have been output-ted by your network security devices (such as the Routers, Firewalls, Network Intrusion Devices) will literally be your "best friends" when it comes to showing you the trends of wherever there have been signs of malicious or rogue behav-ior. But, depending on how many of these network security devices that you actually have, it can be a time-consuming and laborious task to analyze all of them. Therefore, you should use an artificial intelligence or machine learning–based software package to quickly analyze them and to provide you with the alerts when something is off from the baseline profile.

9. Implement the Zero Trust Framework: In cybersecurity, the traditional model has always been the "perimeter security" approach. This simply means that there is only one line of defense that is surrounding the entire business. While this may have worked in the past, it will not any more. For example, if the cyberattackers were to break through this one line only, then he or she will have free reigns to take over completely your IT and network infrastructure. Therefore, the best approach would be to implement what is known as the "zero trust framework". This is where your entire IT and network infrastructure are segmented into different zones, which is also known techni-cally as "subnetting". Each zone will now have its own layer of defenses, using what is known as "multifactor authentication", or "MFA" in short. This is where at least three or more differing authentication mechanisms are used to confirm the identity of the end user wishing to gain access to the datasets. By tak-ing this kind of approach, while there is a good chance that the cyberattacker can break through the first layer, the chances become almost statistically zero that they will ultimately reach the databases which house your datasets, because of all of the other layers of authentication that they must go through.

10. <u>Always Stay Updated</u>: It is always important for you and your IT security team to keep abreast of the latest happenings with regard to the tenets and provisions of the GDPR and the CCPA. Although this can once again prove to be a very time-consuming task, in this particular case, it is always a good idea to retain an attorney who specializes in the data privacy laws, and from, they can then keep you updated as necessary in terms of what is relevant to your business and datasets.

Finally, all of these steps can be seen in the following illustration:

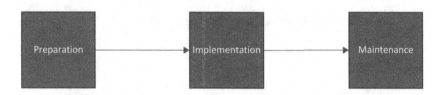

1. <u>Preparation</u>: This is where you and your IT security team take the needed time to fully understand the datasets and where they are or will be located. Also, this is where you conduct the risk assessment study and create the plans as to how you will deploy and implement the needed controls to safeguard the datasets.

2. <u>Implementation</u>: This is where you and your IT security team will put the plans created in the last phase into action.

3. <u>Maintenance</u>: This is the phase where you will be conducting further risks assessment studies to determine and remediate any further gaps and weaknesses that were not discovered before. The primary tools used here will be that of penetration testing and/or vulnerability scanning. Also, this is the step where you and your IT security team will keep a close on the controls that are safeguarding the datasets, and either further optimize or upgrade them as needed. Also, this is the phase where you will need to assess the rights, privileges, and permissions assigned to each and every employee, and making sure that the concept of "least privilege" is being followed, as reviewed throughout this book.

Finally, with many nations around the world and each of the fifty states here creating their own versions of a data privacy law, there is bound to be a lot of confusion and ambiguity as to which ones need to be followed. Therefore, there have been calls now to create what is known as a "Department of Cybersecurity", much like how the "Department of Homeland Security" was created right after 9/11. By taking this particular approach, there will be a degree of centralization, thus creating one set of best practices and standards that all nations can follow.

Resources

1. https://transcend.io/blog/data-mapping-basics

Index

Pages in *italics* refer to figures.

Printed in the United States
by Baker & Taylor Publisher Services